TANGLING WITH THE LAW

REFORMS IN LEGAL PROCESS

Other titles in The Reform Series

*

J. P. Mackintosh

THE DEVOLUTION OF POWER:
Local Democracy, Regionalism and Nationalism

Stephen Fay

MEASURE FOR MEASURE:
Reforming the Trade Unions

Dewi Morgan

THE CHURCH IN TRANSITION:
Reform in the Church of England

THE REFORM SERIES

Tangling with the Law

REFORMS IN LEGAL PROCESS

F. A. R. BENNION

1970

CHATTO & WINDUS
CHARLES KNIGHT
LONDON

Chatto & Windus Ltd.,
Charles Knight & Co. Ltd.
London

*

Clarke, Irwin & Co. Ltd.
Toronto

SBN 7011 1590 4 (hardcover)
SBN 7011 1591 2 (paperback)

Printed in Great Britain by
R. and R. Clark Ltd.
Edinburgh

To
JOHN
who handles so well my
own entanglements

Contents

I

Getting Involved

A person starting to read this book, if he is a layman, may feel himself fairly safe from entanglements with the law. He is, let us say, a good citizen who does his job, pays his taxes, looks after his family and keeps out of the way of trouble. He prefers, like most people, not to 'get involved' and adopts a maxim lawyers in their secret hearts know to be the soundest ever invented: never litigate. What then has he to fear from the law? The reader who is a lawyer, or a layman not lucky enough to have escaped entanglement, would tell him that the toils and tangles of the law cannot always be evaded. Most individuals become involved in major legal process at some time in their lives; many have several encounters with the law; some unfortunates become resigned to being almost constantly at the receiving end of legal activity.

The law is the body of rules laid down by society to govern what we may do to others and they to us. We live in a just society, and on the whole these rules try to be just. They do not always succeed. Even when they do the results may not be to our liking. Furthermore this body of rules is growing all the time, as the state takes on the regulation of every aspect of our life. From cradle to grave, at home, at work and at play, the individual is enmeshed in an ever-growing web of regulations. Most of them are unknown to him, in detail and often in principle. Many are broken constantly, and with impunity. Even so the instances where he cannot avoid tangling with the law multiply as the tangles increase.

We may distinguish, when thinking of law, between substance and procedure. 'Thou shall not kill' is a substantive rule; what happens to you if you break it is a procedural matter. Whatever substantive rules the law adopts are usually brought home to the citizen through procedural steps taken by civil servants, police officers, court officials or other employees of the state. In this book we are not concerned with substantive rules, but with the points where legal procedure impinges on the individual and where large inroads may be made upon his time, his property and his peace of mind. Because it governs how substantive rules work out in practice, procedure is of great importance to the individual.

A substantive rule will tell us when we owe money; procedure tells us what will happen to us if we do not pay, how we can get advice on the problem, whether our property may be forcibly seized, whether, even, we may be sent to prison. By substantive rules our children are prohibited from playing truant, or stealing apples, or drowning the neighbour's cat. Procedure lays down how if guilty they will be dealt with, whether the parent can be made to pay, when they will be sent away to a reformatory or approved school, what rights of appeal there are. Moreover procedural rules are continually being clamped on the ordinary activities of law-abiding people. If you think of starting your own business there will be hosts of formalities to go through. You must get planning permission to use your premises for business purposes; you must comply with the Companies Acts, the Building Regulations, the law governing employment of staff, the Tax and National Insurance Acts, and all the provisions regulating your particular branch of business–Shop or Factories Acts, licensing provisions and so on. You will have to make all kinds of returns, and submit to all kinds of inspections–every one authorised by some statute or other. If you have any time left to build up your business you will deserve to succeed.

In the modern state procedural law grabs us at birth, and requires that event to be registered by an official. It does the same at death; and in between its requirements are seldom relaxed. We cannot here go into the merits of these things, or sigh for a simpler age. What we propose to do is take a close look at some aspects of legal process and at reforms currently being made or suggested. If law is to be at our elbow at every stage and in every walk of life it should at least appear in a guise which does not needlessly cause us distress or impoverishment. Unhappily we are a long way from that desirable state of things.

There are broadly two ways in which the process of tangling with the law may begin. The first is where the initiative is taken elsewhere, and the subject or victim learns, usually by the service on him of some document, that the wheels of law have started to turn. The document may be a writ or summons, a notice of intended prosecution, a divorce petition, a notice to quit, a subpoena, a rating proposal or a notice to treat. Often it will be a solicitor's letter, stating in cold and formal terms what is afoot. Sometimes the news may be good: a pension entitlement has accrued or a legacy has unexpectedly been left. Even here it is desirable to know exactly where one stands, and the windfall may not always be unaccompanied by anxiety.

In the other type of case the individual himself takes, or wishes to take, the first step. A tiresome neighbour begins to erect a building which will spoil the view, or cuts down boundary trees, or spreads malicious gossip. The landlord fails to repair the roof. The employer gives an abrupt notice of dismissal. Family problems arise: a child is beyond control, the husband runs off with another woman, an elderly relative claims a right of support. Some state organisation behaves unjustly: the telephone bill contains errors, rates are demanded twice over, the education authority refuses admission to a desired school. Or a simple natural event such as a birth or marriage brings unknown legal consequences. The possibilities are infinite; the legal position usually far from clear.

This is the age of large corporations. Where a legal problem afflicts a body like Shell or Unilever, or the British Steel Corporation or London Transport, there may be much expense; but it can be met out of the corporation's large resources. There may be much difficulty in reaching a solution; but the work is done, as part of their job, by the corporation's employees. The same goes for the difficulties of Government departments or local authorities. With the individual it is different. He has to bear the worry, and usually the expense, himself–in his own time and out of his own resources. His task becomes more formidable as society becomes more collectivist, and the number of big corporations arrayed against him increases. His problem demands special attention, but is not receiving it. That is why in the following pages we look at reforms in legal process from the point of view of the individual citizen who would like to see falsified the Shakespearean dictum that 'the world's not thy friend, nor the world's law'. The unknown is often regarded as an enemy, and our scrutiny is first directed to the citizen's problem of knowing the rules by which his life and property are regulated.

2

Presumed to Know?

It is often said that every citizen is presumed to know the law. Yet instances abound of the widespread ignorance of legal rights and duties. The problem is not new. When Sampson, of the house of Capulet, was challenged by a quarrelsome Montague: 'Do you bite your thumb at us, sir?' he asked his friend Gregory whether the law was on his side if he said yes. On being advised that it was not, his prudent answer was, 'No, sir, I do not bite my thumb at you, sir, but I bite my thumb, sir.' We cannot go through life with a learned friend at our elbow; and even if we could he would lack, in the state of our modern law, the ready response of a Gregory.

The law reports contain many examples of ignorance by the public of elementary law. Most people might be thought to know what constitutes adultery, yet witnesses before the courts in recent years have demonstrated that this is not so. 'I did not think it was adultery during the daytime' was one answer, while a female witness claimed to believe that the term referred to drinking with men in public houses. Others have expressed the view that there can be no adultery unless a child results, or where the woman was over fifty.

People injured in accidents often demonstrate woeful ignorance, regarding themselves as fully compensated if their employer continues paying wages while they are off work recuperating, or, even where they seek recompense for physical injury, being unaware of the right to recover damages for intangible factors like mental distress or loss of the faculty to enjoy physical exercise. Myths arise as to the consequences of invoking legal process, as that where a tenant applies to the rent officer for the fixing of a fair rent, this gives the landlord the right to evict him. The Molony Committee on consumer production found that many people did not know of the law's protection for the shopper, being ignorant, for example, that reasonable fitness for purpose and merchantable quality are implied where there is no written agreement. Again, there is general unawareness that in most cases legal duties to the purchaser are imposed on the retailer rather than the manufacturer. It is needless to multiply examples; the plain fact is that while the law works on the basis that its precepts are known to the citizen, in doing so it is founded on an obvious lie.

THE FORM OF THE LAW

It is a paradox of modern life that we are governed by a set of rules which most of us can have no expectation of being able to master, or even comprehend in outline. Indeed few citizens, apart from professional people and officials, have any clear idea of the form in which the law is embodied or the machinery by which it is altered. In Britain the law is divided into case law, expressed in reported decisions of the judges; and statute law. If any dispute is brought before the courts the judge has to decide it: he cannot say that the law is not clear and refuse to give judgment. Over the centuries this principle has meant the evolution of legal rules on the basis of court decisions. By now there are more than 300,000 reported cases. Most have ceased to be relevant, but a conscientious lawyer seeking to advise a client may have to search through a great many of them. Often they are exceedingly long – a report of a single case may exceed the length of this book – and their meaning and current significance can only be extracted by painstaking and time-consuming effort. Few places outside London have a comprehensive law library, and in the absence of this the practitioner's task becomes very difficult.

The increasing concern of Government with every detail of social and economic life has led to an enormous growth of statute law during the past century. An Act of Parliament overrides case law, and indeed any previous inconsistent Act. Apart from the thousands of Acts currently in force, there is an even greater volume of delegated legislation – rules, orders and regulations – made by Government departments under powers conferred by Act of Parliament. The combined mass is known as statute law, and as a distinguished judge recently remarked: 'The Statutes are elaborate to the point of complexity: detailed to the point of unintelligibility; yet strangely uninformative on matters of principle.'

Apart from these formal sources of law, there are numerous expressions of official policy which, although not having the force of law, have the effect of it. This is because it is seldom sensible to disregard such statements. Examples are Ministry circulars and memoranda explaining official policy in administering an Act, lists of extra-statutory concessions published by the Inland Revenue and white papers and other expressions of policy which the Government expects to see observed. While Government wishes are not law they often, particularly in the economic field, have just as much effect as law and may even be obeyed more comprehensively than formal legal rules backed up by criminal penalties.

HOW LAW IS MADE

The processes of law making generally take place in public. The decisions of the judges are given in open court, and arise out of issues publicly argued during the court proceedings. Acts of Parliament only become effective after public proceedings which are fully reported in all their stages. This means that the diligent student of current affairs can learn of new legal developments as they occur–at least where they are of major importance. With Acts of Parliament he even has a chance of altering the outcome through writing direct to his Member of Parliament. M.P.s are very sensitive to this means of pressure, the volume and extent of which is an accurate guide to public opinion.

Case law, as we have said, is made by the judges. There is a hierarchy of courts, topped by the House of Lords. The weight and importance of judicial decisions varies with the status of the court. Until recently, when the rule was changed, decisions of the House of Lords were binding even on that Court unless altered by Act of Parliament. Now that this is no longer so the difficulty of ascertaining the law is increased, since even if the highest tribunal in the land has firmly stated a rule there is no guarantee that this statement will not be departed from in a future case. Another complicating factor is that in the appeal courts (including the House of Lords) several judges decide a case, and each may deliver his own judgment. The case may be decided by a majority, but even where the judges are unanimous they may not all give the same reasons and the task of deciding precisely what rule of law is laid down by the judgment can be exceedingly difficult. Furthermore judicial law is seldom made in comprehensive fashion; judges prefer to confine their judgments to what is necessary to decide the dispute before them. Generalisations from specific decisions are left to textbook writers and other commentators.

The position is different with statute law. Here at least general rules are laid down, and the position is not complicated by consideration of a particular set of facts. The field occupied by statute law is continually growing, and the official objective is ultimately to embody all law in this form. It was not always so. Tudor statutes were so few that it was possible for the monarch to do some at least of his own drafting. Henry VIII did this, which must have made commentators less ready to criticise the results than they are today. At the close of one parliamentary session Queen Elizabeth I asked the Speaker what its Members had passed. 'An it please your Majesty', he replied, 'we have passed two months and a half.'

Most modern Acts of Parliament originate in a Government department. The Minister in charge of the department brings forward legislative proposals to his Cabinet colleagues, and if they approve the draftsman is instructed. All Acts of Parliament which form part of the general law and do not relate exclusively to Scotland are nowadays drafted in the Office of Parliamentary Counsel to H.M. Treasury. This Office was established by Robert Lowe, Chancellor of the Exchequer, in 1869. Hitherto most Government Bills had been drafted in Lincoln's Inn as part of the ordinary work of Chancery barristers. Lowe's object was 'to have a considerable drafting department and thus to train up young men in this very peculiar branch of business'. Nowadays the Office consists of around eighteen lawyers, together with supporting staff. Mostly the draftsmen work in pairs, and the number of Bills produced annually approaches a hundred. The senior of the pair handling a Bill takes full responsibility for it. This covers not only the drafting of the Bill, but the drafting of all amendments made to it during its Parliamentary progress, and the giving of advice to Ministers and Parliamentary officials as to matters arising in the course of its passage. For any major Bill the drafting process may take anything up to a year, with successive drafts being circulated for comment among those concerned. Often as many as twenty successive drafts are printed and circulated in this way before the Bill is first published. Although nominally officials of the Treasury, the draftsmen are responsible on legal points to the Attorney-General. Nevertheless they retain a very real control over the style of drafting, the extent to which matters are spelt out in detail, the use of legislation by reference, the degree to which powers are delegated to Ministers and indeed every aspect of statute law. Statute law today is what Parliamentary counsel have made it. Its virtues and defects reflect their own, and their responsibility is correspondingly great.

Sub-legislation made under delegated powers contained in Acts of Parliament forms in bulk the largest part of statute law. Powers are delegated in this way where the subject matter is comparatively trivial, or is constantly fluctuating. Import duties, for example, are changed frequently and the entire Customs Tariff is made and maintained under delegated powers. Although exercisable by a Minister of the Crown, the powers are usually subject to Parliamentary control. Mostly this takes the form of the right of either House of Parliament to annul an instrument – though without affecting anything done under it before annulment. In a few important cases, notably where an instrument imposes a tax, it cannot be effectively made until Parliament has given specific approval. Rules, regulations and orders of this kind are known as statutory instruments and published in a special series.

Finally we should mention private and local Acts of Parliament. These are drafted by Parliamentary Agents and enacted by a special process involving the publication of notices in the locality affected and the hearing of objections. These Acts are often secured by local authorities to supplement their powers under general law. In such cases the citizen living or carrying on business in the area of the local authority is subject to special rules of whose existence he is probably unaware (until he contravenes them) and whose content he will find it very difficult to discover.

BLOODY BOOK AND BITTER LETTER

The Duke in *Othello* might have been referring to the British Statute Book as it is today when he said to Brabantio:

> '. . . the bloody book of the law
> You shall yourself read in the bitter letter . . .'

Dissatisfaction with the state of our statute law is expressed continuously, vociferously and on all sides. The judges vie with each other in the strength of their remarks. One said recently: 'To reach a conclusion on this matter has involved the Court in wading through a monstrous legislative morass, staggering from stone to stone and ignoring the marsh gas exhaling from the depths. I regarded it at one time as a slough of despond, through which the court would never drag its feet; but I have, by leaping from tussock to tussock as best I might, eventually, pale and exhausted, reached the other side.' The draftsman is the main target of criticism, as emphasised in the following gibe:

> I'm the Parliamentary Draftsman,
> I compose the country's laws,
> And of half the litigation
> I'm undoubtedly the cause.'

In one case Lord Justice Scrutton said: 'I regret that I cannot order the costs to be paid by the draftsmen of the Rent Restrictions Acts, and the members of the Legislature who passed them, who bear responsibility for the obscurity of the Acts.'

The legal and other practitioners who have to apply statute law are loud in their complaints. In 1966 a petition was sent to the Minister of Land and Natural Resources which read: 'We the undersigned, being solicitors, accountants, architects and surveyors practising in the city of Birmingham and the Midlands area consider that the Land Commission Bill is too complex in its present form and as we find it impossible to advise our clients we ask that the Bill be deferred.' One practising architect later made a plea for a National Building Act embodying all legislation affecting the design and construction of buildings. He pointed out that there were some 179 national Acts of Parliament which impinged on building operations and at least another 220 local Acts that imposed some measure of control on the construction of buildings. Although the different bye-laws of some 1,400 local authorities have recently been replaced by uniform building regulations, these have been much criticised. The architect mentioned above commented on these regulations: 'The number of technical man hours which have been spent in puzzling out and discussing the meaning and implication of many of the clauses must have been sufficient to have designed and erected many new buildings. Why must we continue to suffer this drag on productivity? There is no reason at all.'

The complexities of tax law are a frequent target. Demanding the setting up of a Select Committee of Parliament to consider the matter, the Chairman of the British Insurance Association said that our taxation laws were now so complicated they imposed an onerous burden on all industries in terms both of time and expense. Law publishers have joined in the chorus. One of them mentions an example of bad drafting brief enough to be given here. By Section 139 (2) of the Transport Act 1968 a definition is given of the phrase 'direct access' as used in the Act. The definition is:

> 'Direct access' means access otherwise than by means of a highway which is not a special road and 'indirect access' means access by means of such a highway as aforesaid.

The critic remarks with some justification that it is difficult to see why the definition was not worded:

> 'Direct access' means access by means of a highway which is a special road, and 'indirect access' means access by means of a highway which is not a special road.

Members of Parliament themselves have admitted defeat. In a debate on the Land Commission one M.P. said that he was delighted to admit that he found it difficult to get beyond the title of the Act. In the other House this was echoed by the Lord Chancellor himself, who frankly said, 'I would be the last person to say that I understand the Bill'.

Apart from the drafting and arrangement of Acts of Parliament, difficulty is often caused by the method of bringing Acts into force and the system of publication. In one case Lord Chief Justice Hewart allowed an appeal against a conviction under an enactment which was found never to have been brought into operation. Although passed by Parliament, it required, by a special provision, the making of an Order in Council before it could become operative. The Lord Chief Justice commented that this was the sort of device which taught us that 'we must venerate that which we cannot presently comprehend in the Constitution'. Even worse trouble occurred in one former Colonial territory where a Spirits Act was not brought into operation owing to forgetfulness by those concerned. The consequences became so involved that a special Act had to be passed to put the matter right. It did so in the following terms:

> 9. (1) In consequence of the provisions of this Act the following enactments are hereby repealed-
>
> (a) the Excise (Amendment) Ordinance 1957 (which shall be deemed not to have amended the Excise Ordinance 1953);
>
> (b) the Excise (Amendment) Act 1958 (which shall be deemed never to have had any effect at all); and
>
> (c) the Spirits (Distillation and Licensing) Act 1959 (which was never brought into operation).
>
> (2) The Excise (Spirits) Regulations 1958 are hereby revoked and shall be deemed never to have been made.

The situation in Britain is greatly exacerbated by the appalling state of the official publications of statute law. In the Third Annual Report of the Law Commission it was admitted that the official edition of the statutes was in 'a sad state', and was no longer obtainable in its entirety because one volume was out of print. The Report justly comments, 'It is not too much to say that this official edition is now in disarray'.

The position regarding publication of reports of cases is rather better. There is no difficulty in obtaining a comprehensive set of official reports, though these run to many hundreds of volumes. The practitioner also has to cope with a number of other series of law reports, of varying quality. The standard nowadays is high, but this was not always so and on some points of law it may be necessary to go back to reporters like Espinasse, of whom one judge irritably remarked that he didn't wish to hear citations from Espinasse 'or any other ass'. It was of a report of this quality that Chief Justice Hope remarked in 1704, 'See the inconveniences of these scambling reports: they will make us appear to posterity for a parcel of blockheads.'

The hazards of case law usually arise from the judges themselves. In the history of the law it has not been uncommon for a judge to deliver a decision and change his mind later. When a case was cited to him, Mr. Justice Maule once said that it was a decision by two judges only; 'and one of them has since repented of it'. In another case Baron Bramwell was confronted with a previous decision of his own but brushed it aside with the remark, 'The matter does not appear to me now as it appears to have appeared to me then.' Instances of this kind are perhaps unavoidable since appeal judges are often faced with cases where the contending arguments are nicely balanced. The layman will have little sympathy with Lord Mansfield's observation that it would be very hard on the legal profession if the law were so certain that everybody knew it. More agreement will be felt for his Lordship's continuation: 'the misfortune is that it is so uncertain, that it costs much money to know what it is'. Lord Chancellor Gardiner's recent feat in persuading the House of Lords to abandon the rule that its decisions bind it until reversed by Parliament is likely to add to the problem. As Chief Justice Black once said: 'The uncertainty of the law – an uncertainty inseparable from the nature of the science – is a great evil at best, and we would aggravate it terribly if we could be blown about by every wind of doctrine, holding for true today what we repudiate as false tomorrow.'

'NO WISER THAN A DAW'

Enough has been said to show that the presumption stated at the beginning of the chapter, that every citizen knows the law, is nonsense. Indeed some judges have accepted that it is nonsense. Lord Justice Scrutton once wrote: 'The fact is that there is not and never has been a presumption that everyone knows the law. There is the rule that ignorance of the law does not excuse, a maxim of very different scope and application.' It is, with respect, difficult to see that this restatement of the rule involves much distinction in practice, though it is undoubtedly a more sensible statement. Either way there is a clear duty on the organs of state to ensure that so far as humanly possible the law is so expressed and published as to come to the knowledge of the citizens who have to obey it. As the Society of Labour Lawyers recently pointed out in a report entitled *Justice for All*, a society which relies heavily on law as an instrument both of social order and reorganisation, including the redistribution of wealth, has a duty to ensure that its members are enabled to conduct their lives within the law. At least the law should be in a state their professional advisers can cope with. Even these nowadays are often forced to echo Warwick's complaint that 'in these nice sharp quillets of the law, Good faith I am no wiser than a daw'.

PROPOSALS FOR REFORM

There is in Britain today a greater volume of law, in a less organised state, than ever before. What is being done about it? In terms of actual accomplishment, very little. This is a period of research and preparation for a determined onslaught on the problem. The neglect of many years has to be overcome, but at least consciousness of the need for improvement now exists among many in responsible quarters–though there remain some strongholds of reaction and indifference.

There is general agreement that the following steps are needed to put the law into comprehensible and acceptable form:

1. Codification of case law.

2. Consolidation of statute law.

3. Presentation of law in a form which brings together all rules relating to a particular subject in up-to-date form.

4. Full development and availability of methods of search and retrieval of laws made possible by computers, and aids to comprehension such as algorithms and flow-charts.

Codification is the process by which legal rules embodied wholly or mainly in reported decisions of judges are reduced to statutory form. In other words the entire law on a topic is extracted from the cases and any relevant statutes and put in one Act of Parliament. To the layman this seems the obvious thing to do, but proposals for codification have rarely succeeded in English law. There are several reasons for this, the main one being that codification is disliked by judges since it puts a brake on the natural development of the law. In an advanced society, however, major changes in law should be effected by Parliament; the courts can be left with a constructive role after codification provided the code is not too minute and detailed. It should leave room for judicial discretion, while avoiding such wide generalisations as to cause inconvenience and uncertainty.

Consolidation is the process of bringing together a number of separate Acts on the same subject into a single comprehensive Act. The earlier Acts are then repealed, and the reader is presented with a 'clean' text. Opportunity is taken to repeal spent Acts, which do not of course need to be reproduced, by a process known as statute law revision.

The body responsible for pursuing the programme of codification and consolidation is the Law Commission, together with the Scottish Law Commission. These bodies were set up in 1965 as the main vehicle for law reform in Britain. With five Commissioners and a staff of fifty, including four draftsmen and fifteen other lawyers, the Law Commission is the most effective body yet established in this country to tackle the huge job of law reform. It has embarked on a programme of codifying four major branches of law: Criminal Law, Contract, Landlord and Tenant, and Family Law. Its consolidation programme is modest. No estimate has been published of the time it would take to produce a complete consolidation of statute law at the rate the Commission is progressing. Indeed progress since the last war has been at a negative rate, well behind the annual output of new statutes.

For many years matters relating to the drafting and publication of statutes have effectively been treated as the entire responsibility of civil servants. Although Parliament has an interest, and a theoretical right to command, it has not played an effective role in these matters. Nor has the Statute Law Committee, an august body which meets only once a year. Parliamentary draftsmen are civil servants employed by the Treasury, and their first concern is to put through Government business in the most effective and expeditious way. Next, they consider the needs of the Members of Parliament through whose scrutiny their Bills must pass. On the publication side, the Stationery Office, again a department of Government and under Treasury control, is protected from the market forces which compel commercial publishers to please their customers or go out of business. With this set-up it is scarcely surprising that the chorus of complaint has gone largely unheeded, and the needs of the user of statute law ignored.

In an endeavour to remedy this state of affairs, and lend support to the Law Commission in its drive for reform, users of statute law got together to form the Statute Law Society in 1968. With three experienced Parliamentarians among its vice-presidents (Lords Shawcross, Stow Hill and Grimston) and a widely representative Council, including Sir John Mellor (Chairman of the Prudential Assurance Company), Sir Henry Wells (Chairman of the Land Commission), well-known lawyers such as Desmond Heap, Frank Layfield and Christopher Slade, as well as a number of accountants, professors of law, and legislative draftsmen, the Council of the Society can fairly claim to be sufficiently high-powered to tackle the problem seriously. The first of the two main objects of the Society is to procure and further the making of technical improvements in the form and manner in which statutes and delegated legislation are expressed and published with a view to making them more readily intelligible. The other main object reflects the need felt by the founders to promote education and research within this field. The Society has begun by appointing a committee of inquiry to assemble and collate the widespread grievances felt by users of statute law. It will then formulate concrete proposals for reform. It has also set up a computer committee to co-ordinate a number of interesting lines of research currently going forward.

The use of computers as an aid to lawyers has reached an advanced stage in the United States under the leadership of John F. Horty, and his methods are being followed in Britain. The object is to put the text of statutes, cases, regulations and other relevant material on magnetic or paper tape, first converting it to computer-readable form. This is fed into the computer, which stores the information in a way which enables searches to be carried out on particular points. Thereafter a properly prepared request will cause the computer to print the legal text required by the person making the search. This saves manual searching through many volumes, and avoids the chance of accidental omissions. Searches can be facilitated by lists of key words in their context, grammatical variants of given words, and vocabularies. In England work on the subject is being led by Colin Tapper in conjunction with International Data Highways, a subsidiary of the International Publishing Corporation which recently took over Butterworths, the law publishers. Other work is being done by Dr G. B. S. Niblett of the Atomic Energy Authority, who has put on computer all enactments relating to atomic energy. Niblett argues that there should be made available to practitioners a service under which electronic-digital computers are used to store, retrieve and index the full text of all legal enactments. Magnetic tape embodying legal texts could also be used for typesetting, and indeed could for a suitable royalty be made available to commercial publishers and others seeking to produce printed editions of statutes and statutory instruments.

Work is also proceeding, particularly at the University of Kent at Canterbury, on alternatives to verbal formulation of legal rules. Hitherto the practice in statutes has always been to express every rule, however complex, in grammatical English. Thus in Acts dealing with taxation or valuation, where arithmetical or even algebraical forms of expression might be more readily comprehensible, the legal principles are spelt out in ordinary language. This perhaps reflects the rule, discussed above, that everyone is presumed to know the law: it is obvious that not everyone knows algebra. The traditional method suffers from grave disadvantages when it tries to lay down rules for an infinitely varying set of circumstances. Some would argue that such rules are better presented in the form of charts, called algorithms, which present a series of alternatives. The individual applying the rules can thus trace his own circumstances right through to a conclusion by adopting the appropriate alternative in each case. While not giving a general picture of the effect of the rules, this is very useful for particular cases.

To remedy the absence of a proper official edition of the statutes, the Statute Law Committee has embarked on the publication of a new revised edition. For the first time the chronological arrangement of the official editions of the statutes will be abandoned in favour of an arrangement chosen according to subject matter. Another innovation is that the edition will be published in the form of booklets for insertion in binders rather than, as hitherto, in bound volumes which can only be kept up to date by sticking in gummed slips and making ink corrections.

Finally there are proposals for improving the quality of drafting itself. Most of these centre on the fact that at present the Parliamentary Counsel have a virtual monopoly of decision on drafting aspects. This is because they are specialists of long experience. In their difficult art, none of their critics can match their expertise. Although there is generalised criticism, therefore, the draftsman is in a commanding position and seldom fails to get his own way on purely drafting points. From time to time suggestions have been made for setting up some kind of supervisory body to check the draftsman's work before Bills are published, or even afterwards. Lord O'Hagan suggested in 1877 that a department to supervise Bills should be established, and in recent times Lord MacDermott, the Chief Justice of Northern Ireland, has proposed that Bills should be scrutinised in draft by a team of 'clause-tasters' who would be without any prior knowledge of the draftsman's instructions. Similarly, Mr Justice Scarman, Chairman of the Law Commission, has suggested the creation of a Department of Justice which would examine the legal quality of Bills at their formative stage–that is before their introduction to Parliament. One reformer, P. De La Cour, has made the interesting suggestion that the electorate would be best served if Parliamentary draftsmen, instead of being civil servants as at present, in future practised their profession on a private enterprise basis. He believes they should practise either alone or in partnership and should be free to accept instructions to draft a Bill from any person or political party prepared to pay for their services. De La Cour optimistically hopes that this system of competition between the draftsmen and payment by results would achieve the desired revolution in the wording of the statutes far more quickly than mere exhortations from politicians unaccompanied by financial incentives.

WILLING THE MEANS

The operation to reform the system of framing and publishing our laws has scarcely got under way. The means are available, but the will is doubtful. Parliamentary counsel are set in their ways, and hardly accept that a problem exists. The Treasury as always are concerned to keep immediate costs down, with little regard for the long-term saving to the nation's economy that could result from a reformed system. Politicians are largely indifferent. It is perhaps significant that of the two Members of Parliament who joined the Council of the Statute Law Society when it was founded, one resigned before the first meeting and the other has not, at the time of writing, put in an appearance.

Nor is there any prospect of a cure for one of the main causes of defective law, namely the haste with which Governments demand legislation. Where the provisions of a law have political significance, there is a likelihood that they will be subjected to frequent change owing to changes in the political complexion of the Government. When such changes come, they will often follow a General Election, and be required at very short notice. If an Act is required to be drafted within a time considerably less than it needs, the result can only be an unsatisfactory piece of legislation. As a well-known Canadian draftsman has said: 'There is for each Bill an irreducible period for preparation . . . as the time is cut down the quality deteriorates so that ultimately the point is reached where no Bill fit for introduction can be produced.' Legislation at the instance of back-bench Members of Parliament can also complicate the law. There has, for example, grown up a practice of having an annual Finance Bill, which itself contains many modifications of tax law, but which has added to it, in the course of its progress through Parliament, a number of further modifications at the instance of back-benchers to deal with what they regard as anomalies in the tax system. Such amendments, often put forward with the best of motives to provide, for example, a particular tax relief for persons suffering from a specific disability, in fact create anomalies of a different kind, since special provision for a special case can only complicate the law.

Another major consideration affecting the clarity of statute law is that reluctance to leave too much to the discretion of officials or the courts leads to over-elaboration. In the case of administrative legislation, there comes a point where the official must be allowed to apply his own judgment to the facts of the case he is dealing with. There is a limit beyond which the legislature cannot, in fact, assert its will. It is a question of great importance where this line is to be drawn, and in this country we have tended, particularly in recent times, to confine administrative discretion within too close limits.

In the field of pure drafting the biggest defect in the present system is the practice of modifying existing law by means of a gloss, rather than a textual amendment. This means that instead of the Act which is being amended having additions or amendments made in its text, so that it continues to be a comprehensive formulation of the law, the amendment is often done in a separate Act not dovetailed in with the earlier one. The reader has himself to do the job of reconciling separate texts instead of having a single amended and unified text presented for his consideration.

Other drafting defects are that Acts contain material required only for purposes of Parliamentary procedure, and make little use of what might be called prefabricated law. By this, common-form provisions are embodied in an Interpretation Act and do not have to be restated each time they are needed. Our Interpretation Act was passed in 1889 and is hopelessly out of date and inadequate. There are thus often endless variations on the same theme (for example, powers of entry or procedure for the service of notices) instead of a single uniform provision applying in all cases. More important, perhaps, is the practice which has grown up over the years of attempting to foresee every contingency and provide for it in considerable detail. The wood and the trees thus become indistinguishable. Comprehensibility is also seriously affected by the frequently-criticised system of legislation by reference. All these objections could ultimately be cured if the will to do so were present. What is needed is a major operation to put the law into acceptable form, and then a sustained drive and determined effort to keep it there. This needs skilled manpower on a scale which is hardly available at present. Each subject of legislation requires to be framed as a single Act. The statute law might be divided into between fifty and a hundred such Acts, each of which would be a comprehensive and properly-arranged statement of the statute law on its own subject. Amendments and future Acts on that subject would be 'slotted in' to the main Act.

The only real objection to this system is that amending Acts would become difficult to interpret in themselves, and Members of Parliament faced with amending Bills might be in difficulty. The remedy is perfectly simple. It is to have a full explanatory memorandum accompanying each Bill so as to explain its effect to Members of Parliament. Such memoranda could also be used by textbook writers and other commentators seeking to explain the effect of amendments. They are quite unnecessary as part of the actual text of the law, and the attempt under the current system to marry the text of the law and commentaries and explanations upon it inevitably produces confusion and added bulk.

Ultimately the responsibility belongs to the Government of the day. Statute law must be taught as a subject in universities, treated as a serious topic for research, and subjected to the disciplines of scientific method. A recruitment drive and training programme for draftsmen needs to be undertaken and the necessary money found. It will not be money wasted if it puts an end to the absurdities of a system under which the legislator defaults on his obligation to maintain a coherent system of law, and leaves it to the user in each case to assemble a jigsaw out of disconnected fragments.

When everything possible has been done, however, there will still remain a large and complicated mass of law. Nothing else is possible in a complex industrial society operating as a Parliamentary democracy. The fiction that the citizen knows the law must, alas, remain a fiction.

3

A Guide through the Maze

THE ADVISORY PROCESS

As we have seen, the average citizen who gets involved, or needs to get involved, in the legal labyrinth cannot be expected to cope with it unaided. If he tries to, he is likely to come to grief. He needs expert advice, and he needs it at the earliest possible moment.

It is worth spending a moment considering the nature of the advisory process. Before sound advice can be given the adviser must learn the facts; and his client may not know them all, and may have got some of them wrong. People are often bad at describing events and things. After an attempted explanation they leave the hearer no wiser, like Antony describing the crocodile as 'shaped like itself, and as broad as it hath breadth'. Or the narrative is directed to one problem, perhaps trifling, while the facts retailed build up, to the acute listener, a different and more vital grievance. Such cases are not always as straightforward as that of the East End housewife who complained of her husband's ill manners in beating her with his hat on. Since the client does not know the law he does not know which facts the law treats as relevant, or that matters felt as burning injustices are sometimes, and with good reason, granted no legal remedy. The adviser needs to be adept in extracting the grains of wheat from the bushels of chaff, and soothing injured feelings.

It is not, however, a mere process of finding the facts and then applying the law to them. The adviser has to bear legal rules in mind throughout the fact-finding process, because only thus can he be sure of extracting the *relevant* facts. Finally, having collected, verified and assembled the relevant facts, he needs to work out the legal consequences and explain them to the client. In Chapter 2 we saw the problems involved, even for an expert, in gaining a comprehensive and accurate grasp of law in present conditions. When these have been surmounted there may still be difficulties in working out the consequences of applying the law to the facts. Even clear rules of law present difficulties when unusual facts arise. In 1954 a cow broke loose from a market in Inverness, got through an unsecured gate, climbed a stair above a shop, fell through the upper floor into the shop and in doing so managed to turn on a tap which flooded the ground floor. The shopkeeper suffered considerable damage, and felt he must have a remedy against someone. But the judge decided, not without difficulty, that 'a gate-crashing, stair-climbing, floor-bursting, tap-turning cow' was a unique phenomenon for which no one could be held responsible.

Clearly the advisory process calls for skill, experience and the expenditure of time. The legal profession feels that other qualities are needed as well: humanity, discretion, impartiality, responsibility and integrity. All these are insisted on by the code of professional ethics. In real terms, sound advice cannot be cheap, even though provided free or at reduced rates. Yet if given early enough it may be less expensive than no advice at all: it may settle a dispute and avoid litigation–especially when coupled with negotiations or conciliation. Litigation has been called the apex of a pyramid whose base is the provision of advice. Traditionally, family solicitors have given wise counsel to their clients (and not only on legal matters) so as to enable them to avoid problems or settle them before they become serious. It is a solicitor's job to *keep* his client out of trouble rather than *get* him out of it. In economic as well as human terms this is a valuable service.

WHERE TO TURN?

If advice is needed, where can it be got? For the affluent there is no problem. A family solicitor, well-versed in his client's history and affairs, stands ready at the end of a telephone. Looked on as a friend, probably of long standing, he takes much of the unpleasantness out of legal entanglements. His advice is not given in cold, abstract terms. Sympathy and resourcefulness, and an identification with the client's interests, give a feeling of support and comfort. Moreover the solicitor will, on an abstruse point, know where to obtain specialist advice–perhaps from another partner in the same firm, or (where the firm is in the provinces) from a London firm. It may be necessary to seek counsel's opinion or to go to other professional people such as accountants or surveyors. Here a knowledge of which practitioners are pre-eminent in their field is vital. In such hands as these, the worried client can relax; his burdens are shifted to other shoulders. There is one condition: he must pay the full economic cost, and in a complex case it will be high. Indeed he may be asked to pay more than this, to make up for his lawyers' losses on clients who cannot afford full fees.

The position is a little different in the middle-income ranges, where there is probably no existing connection with a legal practitioner. A difficulty arises, and advice is needed. Again, the best source is a solicitor but he must be carefully chosen. A recommendation should be sought from a trustworthy and knowledgeable person known to the client–a bank manager or business colleague for example. Fees again will be high, unless the matter is simple.

This then, is the normal and traditional source of advice, but there are many others. Over five hundred Citizens' Advice Bureaux handle nearly two million inquiries a year. Run by the National Council of Social Service, a voluntary body, and largely staffed by voluntary workers, the Bureaux aim to supply the individual with accurate information and skilled advice in many of the personal problems that arise in daily life. They explain legislation and help people to understand and use the many welfare services now available. Only a small proportion of their staff are, however, legally qualified.

Other sources of advice include state officials such as rent officers and probation officers and the other agencies of central and local government, trade unions (for their members), newspaper bureaux such as the *News of the World's* John Hilton bureau (which receives 150,000 queries a year), Members of Parliament (most of whom hold weekly or monthly 'surgeries'), employers, bank managers and many more. A detailed list will be found in Appendix I, together with addresses and telephone numbers. By nearly all these agencies advice is given free. For the poor there are, in addition, the poor man's lawyer services and the official legal advice scheme.

LAW FOR THE POOR

Like the Church of England, the solicitors' profession is often criticised as devised for and manned by the middle classes, who it is said have little or no comprehension of the problems of the poor and respond more readily to middle-class pressures. Professor Harry Street in his *Justice in the Welfare State* complains that in the complex field of 'welfare' legislation there is no specialist legal talent available for the poor, who have nobody to go to for advice. How true is this, and if true how far capable of remedy?

Since 1959 the state has provided an advisory service whereby any citizen with less than £125 disposable capital and less than £7 10*s*. a week disposable income ('disposable' meaning after deduction of necessary items such as housing) can have an advisory session with a solicitor on payment of 2*s*. 6*d*. a half-hour. For those receiving supplementary allowances (formerly national assistance) the session is free. The solicitor is not a state official but a private practitioner, and the interview must be in his office. The actual payment to the solicitor is £1, the extra 17*s*. 6*d*. being paid by the state. Advice may be on civil or criminal matters.

In addition to this official scheme the Law Society runs a voluntary scheme under which a person may, no matter what his means, obtain advice at £1 the half-hour from any solicitor who has joined the scheme. Also available to help the poor are the poor man's lawyer centres and other facilities mentioned on page 25.

The number using the official advice scheme is about 60,000 a year. Five times as many, estimate the Prices and Incomes Board, obtain totally free advice from solicitors who for one reason or another refrain from charging a fee.

IS IT ENOUGH?

The state lays down legal rules. Does it discharge the obligation to ensure that its citizens understand them or at least are advised of their effect? The Society of Labour Lawyers thinks not, and the Society of Conservative Lawyers is inclined to agree. The Lord Chancellor's advisory committee on the legal aid and advice scheme lament an actual fall in the numbers seeking to use the advice scheme, while the Prices and Incomes Board venture the guess that there is a large volume of potential and unrecognised demand for legal advice which, if brought to the surface, might generate a burden of largely unremunerative work for the profession.

We could each benefit from having a benevolent and all-wise adviser always on hand to guide us through the mazes of tax law, to tell us when our piece of bad driving is merely foolhardy and when it constitutes an offence, to explain our remedies against tiresome neighbours, inconsiderate employers or an erring spouse, and to indicate all the benefits and privileges placed at our disposal by the state. None of us get the best treatment theoretically possible – life is too short even for sea-lawyers to claim every right and privilege open to them. But it is said, and probably rightly, that the 60,000 clients of the official legal advice service represent only a tiny fraction of the poorer people who could be greatly, even dramatically, helped by timely advice. The service is there; why do they not use it?

A number of reasons are advanced by reformers. The Labour lawyers hark back to the middle-class image of solicitors: the working man they say, is afraid of looking foolish in the surroundings of a professional office, especially in his working clothes. The solicitor's offices may be some distance away. Even when they are nearby, but in unfamiliar territory, the working man would 'view with horror' the prospect of visiting them. Furthermore, it may be difficult to attend during office hours without loss of wages. Above all there is a fear of law and lawyers born of being always at the receiving end of dunning letters, notices to quit, county court summonses, and the attentions of police and bailiffs. Shakespeare said that in time we hate that which we often fear, and showed it by Jack Cade's cry: 'the first thing we do, let's kill all the lawyers!' The attitude survives, and the Milner Holland Committee on London housing found that tenants of small means had a marked fear and distrust of law and lawyers. For them the law is a thing of expense and delay, and to be shunned.

The Labour lawyers also attribute non-use of the advice scheme to ignorance–both of the scheme itself and what it offers, and also of the very existence of legal rights and remedies or the possibility of them. The Lord Chancellor's advisory committee finds other reasons: the means test is too stringent, the scope of the service too limited, the remuneration of the solicitor inadequate. The Law Society criticise the lack of advice for those who cannot attend a solicitor's office: the bedridden, the prisoners, the hospital patients. On one thing all agree: changes and improvements are needed.

WHOSE RESPONSIBILITY?

We are conditioned nowadays to assume that where an official service is proved inadequate the state is directly responsible for remedying the matter by methods financed out of taxation. We may even, like the Labour Lawyers, assume more or less automatically that the solution must be to set up a new public service, staffed by salaried officials.

That the state has a responsibility for the provision of legal advice to its poorer citizens few can doubt. The Labour lawyers are right to say that a humane and civilised social system cannot fall back on the argument that if people choose not to use a facility offered to them at little or no cost that is their own concern, not society's. We must search out and succour those who for no fault of their own do not come forward to help themselves. The potent misery of our times is felt by those, relatively few, who through lack of initiative, grinding poverty, ill-health or other cause are unable or unfitted to go out and seek a remedy. The state must see that they are helped, but it does not necessarily have to do the job itself.

The traditional providers of legal advice are the legal professions. Their independence of the state (or anyone else) is one of our cherished safeguards, fought for over again in every generation. In a period when legal claims lie more and more against the state or its organs, in step with the spread of state management of our affairs, any innovation should be narrowly scrutinised if it involves the setting up of a state organisation to provide advice. The reasons, transparently obvious, are played down by many or even ignored; so let us briefly examine them.

A legal adviser employed by the state will wish to progress in his career, which he can only do by pleasing his employer (in effect other more senior state officials). He may well *displease* his employer by advising a client that a claim exists for some form of misconduct by other state officials (or even his own superiors). He will therefore be tempted not to give this advice, or to water it down.

This puts the matter crudely. It ignores important side issues such as the loss of independence of mind arising from loss of private-practitioner status, and the effect on other vital professional characteristics such as humanity, the personal approach, and the taking of full personal responsibility for advice given. A thoroughgoing state system substitutes civil service standards of conduct (hierarchical and bureaucratic, serving the ends of Government) for those of the free professions. In turning to look at the remedies suggested let us therefore keep in mind that for the health of the community improvements should come by modifying, and not by supplanting or duplicating, existing professional services.

RIVAL PROPOSALS

How should legal advice be made more readily available, especially to the poor? The argument is between those who think it enough to strengthen the present system and those who want to set up a completely novel organisation.

The Law Society, displaying its consistent desire to keep legal advice primarily in the hands of solicitors in private practice, looks for a solution by amalgamating the official advice and aid schemes so that there is no gap between them, and by making the procedure more informal. Solicitors giving advice would be able to do additional work as well, such as writing letters or drafting documents. Provided the total fee did not exceed £25 no external means test would be applied: the solicitor himself could assess the client's means and according to the result charge him nothing, 30*s*., £3 or £6. The balance would be recoverable from official funds whether the work was done in the solicitor's own office or elsewhere. It is generally agreed, and has been recognised by Lord Chancellor Gardiner, that the income limits for free or assisted legal advice should be raised considerably, but, as with so many reforms, cost is the obstacle.

It is particularly painful to be in prison or other legal custody without recourse to legal advice. The Widgery Committee, reporting in 1966, found that, although the police would not place any unreasonable obstacle in the way of an arrested person who wished to obtain legal advice, in practice his chance of doing so where he had no solicitor and insufficient means was 'remote'. He would probably not know even that the official advice scheme covered criminal matters, and it was nobody's job to tell him. The Committee recommended that all persons in custody should be given this information, together with a list of available solicitors. A solicitor visiting a client in custody should be allowed to charge for his travelling time and expenses. The idea of having permanent legal advisers at prisons was however rejected on the quaint ground that there would be a danger of prisoners later receiving conflicting advice from an outside solicitor assigned to represent them in court. Also rejected was the proposal that a rota of solicitors on the legal advice panel should be on night call to help persons inconsiderate enough to get arrested after office hours. This would be 'liable to abuse'. 'We believe', added the Committee, 'that even a person with ample means to engage a solicitor privately would usually find it difficult to persuade one to visit him at a police station late at night except possibly for the most serious offences. . . .' This startling view of the way the profession regards its duty is, let us hope, unfounded. Since most who are arrested appear in court next morning their need for immediate advice in all but trivial cases is obvious. And there is always the telephone.

The Society of Labour Lawyers advocates the duty lawyer system, under which solicitors on the legal advice panel would attend County Courts and Magistrates' Courts to give advice to persons involved in court proceedings. This was rejected by the Widgery Committee in relation to Magistrates' Courts as being impracticable because of the large number of courts (over a thousand) and wasteful since the services would not always be required. With justification the Labour Lawyers attack this negative attitude and ask for the idea to be tried in some of the busier courts.

The present system of advice should, say the Lord Chancellor's advisory committee, be improved in the voluntary sector as well. The Citizens' Advice Bureaux should be strengthened, and encouraged to become the main source of preliminary or 'non-legal' advice for the ordinary citizen. Private-practice solicitors should attend Bureaux for advice sessions on a rota system.

Subsidies to improve the distribution of solicitors' offices are advocated by the Society of Conservative Lawyers:

> We should seek to attract lawyers to poorer areas and overcome regional shortages of solicitors by making practice in these areas financially more attractive. We propose the payment of capital grants to persons starting practice as solicitors within appropriately designated areas. Alternatively, the grant could be in kind, for example, the provision of premises. In addition we suggest that all solicitors practising in these areas should be paid for their legal work at a higher rate than in the rest of the country. . . .

This strange suggestion, which would be extreme even from doctrinaire socialists, can scarcely be taken seriously. The reluctance of the poor to travel to town centres for advice (if it really exists) must be overcome, but not by bribing the mountain to go to Mahomet. Publicity, coupled with payment of travelling expenses where necessary, should meet the case.

Finally in this brief survey of suggestions to improve the existing advisory services both official and voluntary, we consider the Law Society's proposal for setting up a liaison service to link the legal advice scheme, the private practitioner, and the voluntary agencies such as the Citizens' Advice Bureaux. The suggestion is that the salaried solicitors who administer legal aid on behalf of the Law Society in each area should be augmented so that they can spend some time 'in the field'. They would thus be available to give legal advice at voluntary bureaux, to instruct social workers, and give some cohesion to the present rather ramshackle system. They could also perform the useful function of ensuring that advisory facilities were known to all in the area who might need them.

NEIGHBOURHOOD LAW CENTRES

Is it enough to make improvements in the existing advisory system? The Society of Labour Lawyers think not. Turning their eyes across the Atlantic, they advocate a new system based on the neighbourhood law firms in the United States. It is important to grasp what this American innovation is, and what it is not.

There are about a thousand neighbourhood law firms, located in almost every State of the Union. They are situated in the slums or other poor areas, and although financed largely from Federal taxation, each is an independent entity under the control of a local Board of Trustees comprising representatives of the local Bar, law teachers, legal practitioners in private practice and representatives of the poor. The Board supervises the operation of the NLF and employs the salaried lawyers who run it. Salaries are a little lower than those paid in private practice, but the tradition is growing under which it is regarded as a duty for young lawyers to work in an NLF for a time as a form of social service. In this way, a number of brilliant law graduates have been recruited to the service, if only temporarily. Many University Law Departments have started their own NLF as an adjunct to teaching and research programmes. The independence of each NLF is demonstrated by the fact that there is no uniformity in the test of means applied; this is one of the many matters left to each Board to decide for itself.

The main function of the NLF is to provide a legal advisory service to the lower income groups. Where a client appears to have a claim for substantial damages he is passed on to an ordinary law firm, since under the American system of contingent fees the lawyer would charge a fee only where it could be met out of the proceeds of a successful claim.

The NLF system is conceived as part of the war on poverty and promoted by the Office of Economic Opportunity. It has wider aims than the mere provision of legal advice. It seeks to make the poor aware of their legal rights by using positive methods. It helps law reform by initiating test cases, promoting legislation and pressing for the alteration of unjust administrative procedures. It tries to make the NLF an integral part of the community, and thus gain acceptance for law and lawyers.

The poor are encouraged to form pressure groups similar to those commonly found in the higher reaches of society, and the system attempts to further their participation in social life. It flourishes alongside a system similar to our own legal advice service (though of limited scale) known as Judicare. The NLF system has the advantage that most of its practitioners deal exclusively with cases grounded in poverty, and become expert in the special techniques required. A Harvard study found that the fees of lawyers under Judicare raised the cost to two or three times that of the NLF system. Although the latter involves administrative overheads which have to be directly borne, the lawyer's fee takes account of his own overheads and also a profit element.

The NLF system has been supported by the American Bar Association, but only because it is satisfied that the programme is run on professional lines which do not jeopardise the independence and traditions of the Bar. It can be seen that the American NLF performs a highly useful social function and does so without imperilling the public's right to have recourse to a legal profession totally independent of the state. The scheme proposed by the Labour lawyers for this country is very different.

The system of local law centres proposed by the Labour lawyers would be under the control of a national board on which representatives of the legal profession would be in a small minority. The sponsors insist that the system must have its own identity and values, with a new leadership freed from traditional moulds. For this reason they explicitly reject the idea that the Law Society should run it as it runs the Legal Aid and Advice Service. Instead of the autonomy enjoyed by each NLF in America, the local law centre would be controlled by the national board through a local executive committee consisting of the staff of the centre and members of the local community. Local law societies would not be represented. The full cost of the new system would be met by the Exchequer–again departing from the American pattern under which a proportion of the cost has to be provided by local contributions or in the form of voluntary work. Another departure is the recommendation that there should be no means test. This is contradicted later by the suggestion that those working in the centre should have a clear rule that anyone who can obtain the help he needs from the ordinary facilities ought to be told to use them and sent away. This is an example of the muddled thinking which characterises the proposal. It is obvious that the practical working of the centre requires either that there is a clear means test or that it must be open to all. The idea that in a state-financed service a taxpayer helping to finance it should be told to go away because an official, acting presumably by intuition, thinks he can afford an ordinary solicitor is unacceptable.

The proposal excludes certain types of work from the ambit of a local legal centre. It should undertake no conveyancing or, with some exceptions, litigation. The exceptions include the case where there is urgency, as where a County Court summons is to be heard next day, and those where legal aid is not available, such as representation before a tribunal. Centres are not to be prohibited from acting on both sides in a dispute. The proposers somewhat vaguely hope that through specialisation and economies of scale the centre would be able to operate more economically than a firm of private practitioners. Other hopes are that the service could attract law graduates who would find private practice insufficiently rewarding, and that establishment of the Centres would significantly improve the image of the legal profession as a whole, and would produce a general improvement in recruitment.

OBJECTIONS TO LOCAL LAW CENTRES

The proposal to establish local law centres has attracted little support. The Law Society see it as the thin end of the wedge, leading to loss of professional independence and a total nationalised legal service. The Society of Conservative Lawyers take the same line:

> Lawyers paid, instructed and employed by the State will work for, act for and look to the State and and not to their clients for their future. If the State takes over the lawyers, who will fight the State?

The Lord Chancellor's Advisory Committee is not satisfied of the need for such a radical and expensive new scheme, and would prefer to improve existing services. The scheme is even contrary to evidence given by the Labour Party to the Rushcliffe Committee in 1945 opposing the setting up of legal advice bureaux by the state. The Labour Party said that there were 'obvious objections' to these, not the least being state involvement in many legal claims. These objections remain valid.

The local law centre proposal is a typical illustration of reformer's grandeur. The professional reformer is not content with modest improvements in an existing system; these are dismissed as 'tinkering'. Any public money going must be used to build a bright new structure, which will make good newspaper copy and may be taken up as a politician's package–one of a tray of goodies used to entice voters at a general election. This besetting drawback of democratic politics has no place here. The citizen's basic rights are at stake, and there is no room for compromise.

Nor is there any room for experiment. *The Times* newspaper artlessly suggested that the only way of evaluating the contradictory arguments over local legal centres was to put them to the proof by setting up pilot projects. The dangers of this are transparently clear. Such projects must be manned by lawyers trained in the present independent philosophy, since there are no others. If, as might happen, their independent outlook surmounted the conformist pressures of the experimental system this would be hailed as the signal for advance towards a universal state legal service. The fact that this would rear its own legal officials, inevitably with different values, would be brushed aside.

The truth is that there is no justification for running the risk inherent in the scheme proposed by the Labour lawyers, even if it were not condemned on other grounds. The risk is neatly exposed in another section of the Labour lawyers' own report which deals with public officials engaged in welfare services:

> It is known that social workers often feel reluctant to take up the cudgels on behalf of clients for fear of antagonizing other public officials. . . . Some social workers have felt for instance that the friendly relations between themselves and the local Ministry of Social Security office would suffer if they encouraged their clients to use the (supplementary benefits) appeal machinery. Child care officers from more than one local authority have reported difficulties even in requesting a written explanation of a supplementary allowance, owing to senior officials' disapproval of such 'militant' action.

Employees of a local legal centre would of course be one type of official social worker and would be likely to display the same aversion to 'militancy' as the rest. It is striking that the fact that they have thus disproved their own case has escaped the authors of *Justice for All*.

Another aspect of reformer's grandeur in its present-day guise is that it nearly always requires the setting up of yet another state board with expensive offices and hordes of officials. Apart from duplicating the Law Society's administrative set-up the proposed national board for local legal centres would suffer from the usual defect of such bodies. Being composed of busy people mainly drawn from other spheres, its real policy would be in the hands of its permanent officials.

Instead of a governing body largely ignorant of the profession, its techniques, standards and limiting factors, how much better to leave the running of legal advice services to people who belong to the profession, know its problems from lifelong experience, and have it as their main interest. The Labour lawyers, in advocating their national board, are not only disloyal to their own profession–

they are turning their backs on an opportunity to improve the service it gives in favour of a novel and unnecessary expedient. We may be sure that if public money were found to operate local legal centres there would be little left over to improve the present legal advice system as well.

It is hardly necessary to state further objections, but two more should be briefly mentioned. The first is that a poor person is now able to consult an ordinary solicitor in his ordinary office; in future he might be forced to go to a centre designed for the poor and inevitably looked on as second-rate. The second, not entirely flippant, is that with such a proliferation of advisory services people would need advice on which advisory service they should use!

WHAT SHOULD BE DONE?

A sensible reformer looks first at the cause of the problem. Almost everyone in Britain today, whatever his income, feels the need for a guide through the legal maze. Before rushing to provide more guides we might do well, as suggested in Chapter 2, to launch a determined onslaught on the maze itself and give up our inclination to add innumerable new complications in every year that passes.

Next, we should insist on the duty of each organ of state having charge of some portion of the maze to explain it to the citizen. The refusal of the Board of Inland Revenue to give advance rulings on tax liability, so that tax payers can know with safety whether a projected course of action is wise, should be reversed. Much is done to publicise and explain welfare services and allowances, but the same attitude does not prevail in other spheres.

Furthermore the state should evolve systems and procedures to ease the citizen's task in coping with its exactions. A man even of modest affairs finds much of his spare time consumed in making returns, keeping accounts, answering official letters, paying bills, and coping with the routines and emergencies of life today. One suggestion to this end, for a uniform computerised system of state-citizen payments, is made in Chapter 7. Other aids could no doubt be devised.

These suggestions, if resolutely carried through, would do something to reduce the need for advice and the real cost of giving it. For the rest, the answer lies in improving the present advisory system and public awareness of it. The Law Society have found that posters put up in local post offices lead to a dramatic increase in applications for free or assisted legal advice in the area. Shortage of funds for adequate publicity has had much to do with under-use of the service.

Should we try experiments on the lines of the American NLF system, but without the objectionable features introduced by the Society of Labour Lawyers in their proposal for local legal centres? Initiatives by local organs of the profession would be welcome, as would experiments by university legal departments. Indeed one such initiative has taken place – in North Kensington. Here an American-style neighbourhood law firm has been set up by a group of lawyers and social workers headed by Muir Hunter Q.C. Provided state control is rigorously excluded, and the legal profession given a commanding role, much good could result from such moves. Lawyers must lead the drive for better services, especially to the poor. They must take notice of the objections levelled by those reluctant to consult them and change their methods where necessary. If they do not they may indeed find themselves bypassed, and later superseded, by some new state organisation. That would be a tragedy, not only for them but for the nation.

4

The Talkative Road to Truth

THE FAIR NAME OF ENGLISH JUSTICE

Good advice, even if made available and acted upon, cannot always save the citizen from finding himself involved in court proceedings–whether civil or criminal. The courts of England have an unequalled reputation for justice. Over the centuries, a number of factors have contributed to the building up of this reputation.

In one of those lawyers' phrases which become familiar to everyone, Lord Chief Justice Hewart said in 1924 that it was of fundamental importance that justice should not only be done, but should manifestly and undoubtedly be seen to be done. The publicity of court proceedings satisfies the parties to litigation, and the public at large, that all is fair and above board. Furthermore the dispensers of justice–judges, counsel and solicitors–have high traditions of integrity, based on the code of professional ethics. Under the English system the judge presides impartially above the arena, he does not descend into the dust and heat of conflict as do his Continental brethren operating the inquisitorial system.

In the field of criminal justice, England's reputation for fairness is supported by the presumption that the accused is innocent until proved guilty, and the exclusion of evidence of his bad character unless, under well-defined rules, he puts this in evidence through his own action. A man is not made to stand trial on a serious charge unless at a preliminary hearing a magistrate has found that there is a case against him. If he has to stand trial he has the noted protection of the jury system.

The popularity of the jury was explained by one American judge as being based on the fact that the individual can forfeit his liberty 'only at the hands of those who, unlike any official, are in no wise accountable, directly or indirectly, for what they do, and who at once separate and melt anonymously in the community from which they came'. The jury system has long been praised. Blackstone looked upon it as the glory of English law, and remarked that 'the liberties of England cannot but subsist so long as this palladium remains sacred and inviolate'. The jury has also been described as 'the foundation of our free constitution', 'the bulwark of our liberties' and 'the lamp that shows that freedom lives'. In less flattering terms it has been called predominantly male, middle-aged, middle-minded and middle-class. Although nowadays mainly thought of in terms of criminal trials, the jury still survives in civil cases. Up till 1854 all civil cases in the courts of common law were tried by juries, and no other mode of trial was available. The only civil cases where there is now a right to a jury are those concerned with fraud, defamation, malicious prosecution, false imprisonment, seduction or breach of promise of marriage. In other cases, a jury will not be permitted unless, exceptionally, the judge gives permission. Otherwise the trial is by the judge sitting alone.

Many other factors contribute to the high reputation of English justice. Complex rules are designed to ensure that the evidence produced to the court is the best available, even if they exclude information which most people would feel it safe to rely upon in their ordinary lives. Every effort is made by the court to protect litigants from surprise evidence or inadvertent failure to observe proper procedure or attend hearings. The appeals system is highly elaborate. From any of the four divisions of the High Court or from the County Court an appeal lies to the Court of Appeal, usually composed of three Lords Justices. From there an appeal may lie to the House of Lords sitting in its judicial capacity. The system of appeals in criminal cases is even more complex.

The English system under which the judge stands apart as umpire or referee rather than inquisitor leads to what has been called the adversary system of our jurisprudence. The responsibility is on each party, or his advocate, to present the best case he can and for the judge as it were to notch up points and give his decision accordingly. The judge is limited in his material to what the parties choose to place before him. He cannot, as under the French system, make his own investigations, call his own witnesses, and ferret for the truth in whichever direction he may think it lies. Furthermore the procedure in England is essentially oral, and in this many problems reside.

English lawyers display a deep-rooted aversion to written evidence even where it is verified by oath, as in an affidavit. The desire always is to hear the witness speak his evidence, to watch his demeanour, to test him by questioning. None of this is possible with typewritten sheets bound in green ribbon. Hence the old gibe 'truth will out, even in an affidavit'.

What has been described as the 'comprehensive orality' of English legal proceedings is truly remarkable. The entire case is conducted by word of mouth from beginning to end. Although there are usually many documents in the case, from correspondence between the parties to the written pleadings in which claim and defence are specified, the judge cannot be taken to have read them beforehand and they must be read out by counsel. So must legal judgments and statutory enactments on which counsel wishes to rely. Even where an affidavit has been sworn it does not become evidence until read out by counsel in court. When judgment is given, even though it has been written out beforehand, it is read by the judge in open court. The justification usually given is that only in this way can the public know what is going on; only thus can justice 'manifestly and undoubtedly be seen to be done'.

TALKING, LISTENING, WATCHING

The purpose of court proceedings is threefold. Where any facts are in dispute between the parties (and this is usually the case) evidence must be heard and the dispute resolved. Then, the facts having been decided, it is necessary to ascertain the legal rules which apply. Here again there may be dispute between the parties, and the court must resolve it. Finally the court must apply the legal rules to the facts, and in the course of doing so exercise any discretion entrusted to it. The law does not automatically give a precise answer; it lays down principles and there is room for variation in their application. One obvious example concerns the sentence to be imposed on a convicted criminal. There are limits beyond which the court cannot go, but within these there is a very wide discretion.

As we have seen, it is the firm view, and the traditional view, of English lawyers that the functions thus described are best carried out orally. This is nowhere more true than in relation to evidence. It is the proud boast of English law that few liars leave the witness box without their lies having been exposed. For the ordinary person, unfamiliar with courts of law, it is almost impossible to carry off a lying story successfully. The strangeness of the surroundings, the curious garments and wigs worn by the judge and counsel, the whole atmosphere of judicial formality, strike chill into the heart of the would-be perjurer. He is not allowed to tell his story in his own way; it has, in the traditional manner, to be extracted from him by a series of questions. He may not have a copy of his proof of evidence to refer to, but must remember the story he has determined to tell. Judges and counsel are well accustomed to detecting the note of falsity, the strained demeanour, which accompanies a lie. Often the judge will intervene with a shrewd question. Counsel for the other side, when his turn comes to cross-examine, can take as long as he likes and put as many questions as he thinks fit. The witness's ordeal can be protracted. In a criminal case, or occasionally in a civil one, the jury watches it all with silent attention. In such an atmosphere, truth will out. A story which on paper may convince, or at any rate give no grounds for suspicion, falls apart in oral examination. Nor should one overlook the demeanour of others present during the testimony. The effect of a piece of evidence upon the prisoner, or upon the parties to a civil action, can be read (perhaps sometimes misread) from a look, a gesture or an exclamation.

Another important element of oral procedure is argument. One side seeks to persuade judge and jury by its presentation of the facts and the law, while the other side seeks to dispel any favourable impression and win conviction for its own point of view. Questions that occur to the judge can immediately be put by him and answered. At times the proceedings may take on the air of a debate, with the thorough unravelling of problems that discussion can bring.

This then is the way of English law, a traditional way of thrashing out points at issue openly, publicly, and–here's the rub–without unseemly haste.

TIME THE ENEMY

Time is the enemy of truth. The number of man-hours required to process a case through to finality can be enormous, and the main reason is undoubtedly the oral nature of court proceedings. There are many aspects of this.

The oral character of a trial means that a large number of people have to be collected together in one place for a period of time. A quite ordinary case may take a day or more to try; some take many weeks. Congregated together during the entire hearing are judges, counsel and solicitors–all expensively trained, whose time is valuable. There may be expert witnesses, also expensively trained. Jurors and ordinary witnesses have to leave their daily work to attend court. Add parties, court officials, solicitors' clerks, members of the press, and shorthand writers and the aggregate in working hours is seen to be very considerable. Nor is personal attendance confined to the trial itself. The system in the High Court lays emphasis on the need for attendance at the offices of the court by the parties or their representatives in order to take any step in a legal action whether before or after the trial.

Then the oral method invites prolixity. The tempo is dictated by the judge, who may be quick-witted or slow, verbose or terse. The late Mr Justice Slade used to complain of being given 'all the long cases' to try, though in fact they did not differ from those allotted to other judges. It was he himself who lengthened them. Although the basic rule for the extraction of evidence is that counsel question the witnesses while the judge and jury listen and watch, judges have been known to take on the role of inquisitor. In one case a conviction was quashed because the judge asked the witnesses 495 questions, whereas the total number asked by counsel for the prosecution and for the defence was only 847. This meant that counsel were unable to present their cases properly since they could not follow a continuous line of questioning. One divorce case went to appeal on the ground that the judge had put to the witnesses many more questions than all the counsel in the case combined. Counsel themselves may be verbose–like the advocate once rebuked by Lord Esher with the remark, 'Time may not be the essence of advocacy, but please bear in mind that in this Court we count in minutes, not days.' A notorious cause of lengthy hearings is the litigant in person. It is a tradition of English courts that the layman who appears on his own account should be given every assistance by the court. Unfamiliarity with procedure inevitably lengthens the trial. So does the human weakness of liking the sound of one's own voice. In a nineteenth-century case for a declaration of legitimacy, which ended in the House of Lords, one of the litigants, a Miss Shedden, addressed their lordships for twenty-three consecutive days!

The presence of a jury retards proceedings. Despite its virtues, a jury is, as Herbert Spencer remarked, a group of twelve people of average ignorance. There is still a property qualification for jury service, but the figures have not been raised to reflect the fall in the value of money and the qualification has become ineffective to exclude the uneducated. Jurors lack experience of court procedure, and the judge has to ensure that the pace is not too fast for the jury to comprehend what is going on. Even so, jurors who have described their experiences subsequently have testified to a lack of awareness bordering on bewilderment. Professor Ely Devons, writing of his experiences as a juryman, criticised the absence of any instructions to the jury about the nature of their function. The clerks and officials treated those summoned to serve as mere 'jury fodder'. The judge went to the other extreme and treated them with great respect and 'almost ostentatious kindness'. In the jury box they were miserably cramped and Devons suffered acutely from the rule forbidding the taking of notes. Nobody told the jury what it was supposed to do, or how it was to go about its task. There was no reasoned discussion of the evidence in the jury room, and Devons concluded that it was just as well that the jury's proceedings should remain secret and that it should give no reasons for its verdict. The influx of Commonwealth immigrants has given further cause for disquiet in recent years. Coming from different cultures, with different values, and often possessing an inadequate command of the English language, they are clearly unfitted to be jurors until they have assimilated English ways over a period of years. Yet the law requires them to be selected for jury service in the same way as the native-born English, and the practice in some places of omitting them from jury lists at the discretion of officials has understandably led to protests.

Criticisms of the jury system as it operates nowadays are not, of course, limited to its effect in drawing out proceedings. There is a strong suspicion that juries acquit the guilty far more often than magistrates or judges would do. Nigel Walker has pointed out that the accused's chances of acquittal vary according to the type of court before which he is tried. Juries acquit in rather more than a third of cases, but magistrates in less than four per cent. Lord Denning recalls how he once summed up to a jury while sitting at quarter sessions. The accused was charged with being in possession of house-breaking implements by night and the judge told the jury that if they thought the accused was at the door at midnight intending to present these implements to the householder as a gift – as a tribute of esteem – then, of course, they would find him not guilty. This was intended as irony in a case where guilt was clear, but to the discomfiture of the judge the jury, no doubt feeling that the possibility offered to them had to be taken seriously, acquitted the accused.

We have mentioned earlier the number of different people required to be collected together for a court hearing. It is obvious that occasions must arise, not infrequently, when some essential person is missing. The judge may be taken ill, or a witness may fail to turn up. It frequently happens that Counsel engaged in the case is also involved in other proceedings elsewhere. The answer to all such difficulties is to adjourn the proceedings to another day, thus dragging them out still further. In one of his *Forensic Fables*, Theo

Mathew touched on this situation in his usual delightful manner. A junior counsel accustomed to practising in the common law courts found himself briefed in a Chancery action. Since he could not understand what the case was about he was comforted to be told that he was to have an experienced Chancery leader to assist him. The fable continues:

> When the case was called on, the common law junior was told by a breathless clerk that the experienced Chancery leader was in the House of Lords and that he was to carry on till the experienced Chancery leader could get back. The common law junior rose to his feet and told the judge in faltering accents that he would read the Affidavits. At first all went well. The common law junior read and the judge followed him attentively. When the common law junior turned over the judge turned over also. But then a hideous event occurred. Towards the end of the third Affidavit the judge suddenly said to the common law junior: 'but how do you get over *in re Puffington's Settlement*?' The common law junior fainted. When he came to himself he was aware that three old gentlemen with beards were asking for costs out of his estate.
>
> Moral–*Ask for an Adjournment.*

The law's delays have long been proverbial, and have long been accepted by English lawyers almost with resignation–if also with exasperation. A nineteenth-century judge once said: 'This case bristles with simplicity. The facts are admitted; the law is plain; and yet it has taken seven days to try–one day longer than God Almighty required to make the world.' Over the past hundred years the delays have been increasing. With the growth of travelling facilities and the making and copying of documents, the amount of evidence, both oral and documentary, has expanded. An additional cause is the abolition of rules preventing parties to civil actions and persons accused of crime from giving evidence on their own behalf. Despite the creation of a large number of additional judges in recent years, the backlog of cases piles up–particularly in the criminal courts. Accused persons may be kept as long as three months in custody before their cases get to court. At the Old Bailey there are always hundreds of cases awaiting trial, even though it now has fifteen courts instead of the four operating just after the war.

CONSEQUENCES OF DELAY

The consequences of delay stemming from the oral nature of judicial proceedings are becoming alarming. They are most manifest in the civil field; in criminal cases accused persons have no option about participating. In civil matters there are two main consequences, both very serious for the maintenance of justice. One is the tendency to bypass traditional legal procedure altogether where new causes of action are being created by Parliament. This has led to the proliferation of administrative tribunals, using simpler procedures, to deal with issues arising under the welfare legislation of recent years. The other consequence is the decision of the citizen himself to bypass the courts by providing for contractual disputes to be settled by arbitration, or simply by declining to litigate even where a good cause of action exists.

Some years ago a top-hatted old gentleman used to parade outside the Law Courts in London carrying a placard saying 'Arbitrate – Don't Litigate'. The advantages of arbitration are that the parties can select an arbitrator who is expert in the matter in question, and can get it dealt with expeditiously. Often the entire proceedings are conducted by means of documents, and all hearings are avoided or at least kept to a minimum. Where they do occur the atmosphere is informal and friendly. Many trade associations keep standing panels of arbitrators expert in the trade. No time then has to be wasted in explaining to the judge necessary background information.

As Lord Devlin has pointed out, it is the decision of people to put up with a grievance, even though the law provides a remedy, which gives rise to most disquiet. Litigation, which ought to be a 'gentle solvent of disputes' has turned into a ruinous luxury. This is because of the protraction of proceedings arising from the fact that English law accepts it as the inalienable right of every litigant to have the whole of his evidence and argument presented by word of mouth–a right recognised only under the English legal system and those derived from it. The resulting cost can never be effectively reduced by such devices as control over lawyer's fees because it is in the main a true cost–caused by taking up the time of people whose time is valuable. Thus individuals feel themselves forced to submit to wrongs because seeking redress for them is an unbearable prospect. Justice is effectively denied, and the unjust flourish. Injustice occurs not in the cases that come to court, but in those that are never brought there. There is something seriously wrong with a society whose judicial processes are regarded by its citizens with profound aversion. Witnesses are reluctant to come forward, for fear of getting involved in the toils of the law. Where they cannot escape, their evidence is often given months or even years after the event, when it has ceased to be reliable. As Mr Justice Paull remarked, no witness can be believed after five years. The period of real reliability is probably much less.

KEEPING COSTS WITHIN BOUNDS

There is an urgent need to reduce the cost of litigation. Since cost is a factor of the man-hours involved this is equivalent to saying that the time needed to arrive at a legal decision must be shortened. How can this be done? 'Justice' (the British section of the International Commission of Jurists) has embarked on a full-scale inquiry into the question, but there have been many previous inquiries and many ideas canvassed. Some of these have borne fruit, but a great deal remains to be done.

If the law were less obscure its operation in a particular case would be worked out in less time, and therefore at less cost. The ways in which the law might be made simpler, and its presentation improved, have been discussed in Chapter 2. Next, some of the elaborate safeguards against error could be relaxed, at least in those civil cases where the subject matter is of no great amount or value. Rights of appeal might be cut down–even abolished altogether where the amount at stake is small. There is much to be said for allowing no more than one appeal in any action and abolishing the appellate jurisdiction of the House of Lords altogether. Appeals from the County Court should go to the High Court, and no higher. Even so, leave to appeal should be required, and granted only sparingly.

In serious criminal cases the preliminary hearing before magistrates might be thought to avoid the waste of time involved in trying people who would ultimately be acquitted. Very few committal proceedings fail however, and the hearing can scarcely be said to act as a sieve. It is probably unnecessary for this purpose, since prosecuting authorities are well able to judge whether a conviction is likely. Committal proceedings are also supposed to help the accused to know what case he will have to meet, but this could be achieved by giving him advance copies of the witnesses' proofs of evidence. Another supposed advantage, the giving of publicity so that unknown witnesses may come forward, carries a corresponding risk of prejudice at the trial. This led to a considerable restriction of press reporting by the Criminal Justice Act of 1967. Reporting is now limited to such formal matters as the name of the accused, a statement of the charge, and the result of the hearing–unless the accused himself asks for wider publicity.

Improvements in the jury system might help to reduce costs. If jurymen were all well-educated and intelligent, had been instructed in their duties and were given facilities for note-taking, they might perform more efficiently. The first improvement is unlikely in these democratic days–indeed it was specifically rejected by the Morris Committee in 1965. The Committee went the other way, and recommended that the only qualification for jury service should be citizenship as evidenced by inclusion in the electoral roll. They would, however, exclude persons over sixty-five and those who have not since the age of sixteen been resident in the United Kingdom. Professor Glanville Williams has advocated trial by three judges instead of a jury, but the problem of recruitment and additional expense is obvious. A better solution would be to expand the roll of lay magistrates and select a smaller jury from them, or use them as judicial assessors. In effect the latter function is already served by lay magistrates sitting at Quarter Sessions with a legally-qualified chairman.

The denial of justice through cost and delay is mainly in the civil field, however, and it is here that further reforms must be strenuously sought. Self-help is distrusted today, but a wider use of remedies like distraint which need no application to the court might be of use. Again, however, the modern tendency, as evidenced by the Payne Committee (page 87 below), is rather the other way. Reforms in court procedure are made from time to time, but on an insufficient scale. Mr Justice Megarry, in his book *Lawyer and Litigant in England*, calls for the complex procedures in the High Court to be simplified on County Court lines. Complaining of the 'greater richness of interlocutory life' in the High Court, where numerous processes to obtain particulars of the pleadings, discovery of documents and so on precede the actual hearing, he praises the less complex, if less perfect, approach of the County Court. By comparison the High Court action is 'a juggernaut proceeding relentlessly from beginning to end, on the assumption that all will have been done impeccably before the case comes into Court to make such a progress possible'. It is 'the Rolls-Royce of procedures: perfect, but damned expensive'. There is indeed little to distinguish the procedure in a small and simple case from that in one that is big and complicated. The result is that it may take a year or more to bring a High Court action to trial, whereas in the County Court a few weeks suffice.

More thoroughgoing reforms are needed however. The adversary system is a cause of delay, even injustice, and requires modification. Treating litigation as a sort of game in which all depends on the efficiency of the performer will not do. The judge needs to play a more active part, to be not merely an umpire but a participant pursuing justice. He should also strive to end the litigation at the earliest possible moment. For this, changes are needed in the conduct of a hearing. Instead of requiring the entire case for the plaintiff to be presented before the defendant can open his mouth, there should be a preliminary stage at which first the plaintiff and then the defendant would outline his case, indicating the evidence to be called. This would enable both sides, and the judge, to form an early view of the likely outcome. The judge might then adjourn briefly and (perhaps in his private room) invite both sides to come together and settle their differences in a just compromise. With such active encouragement from the judge, settlements would be much more common, and the waste of time involved in calling all the plaintiff's witnesses before the defence could judge the strength of his case would often be avoided.

The judge, or the master or registrar acting for him, could be empowered to intervene in interlocutory stages with orders designed to tailor the proceedings to the importance of the issues involved. He might even be authorised in suitable cases to give a decision in chambers with power to exclude legal advisers.

CUTTING THE CACKLE

The reforms we have discussed are substantial. Modifying the adversary system would be fundamental. Yet these changes are not likely to make any dramatic improvement unless the root of the trouble is tackled. With proper safeguards, and in appropriate cases only, the insistence on completely oral proceedings in civil cases must go. As Lord Devlin has said, there will be no worthwhile saving in cost so long as we accept the right of every litigant to have the whole of his evidence and argument presented by word of mouth.

One easy and obvious reform is for judges to read all the papers in a case before the hearing, and for them not to have to be read out by Counsel. To a very limited extent this is done already. In the County Court the judge will usually look at agreed correspondence in advance, and only important letters are read out at the trial. In the House of Lords and the Judicial Committee of the Privy Council it is common on the hearing of petitions for leave to appeal (as distinct from actual appeals) for counsel to be told that their lordships have read the documents and to be asked whether there is anything they wish to add. Mr Justice Megarry, drawing on his experiences at the Bar, shows that this is not always an easy question to answer. Having read the papers, their lordships have probably come to a tentative view. If counsel holds forth to them will he be pushing at an open door, or is persuasion needed? 'The problems of technique are akin to those of trying to tell a long but funny story to an audience which has announced that it has already heard some, if not all, of it but politely inquires whether you wish to make sure they have seen the point.'

Next, the growing tendency to amend rules of evidence so that written evidence is admissible should be encouraged. The Civil Evidence Act 1968 increased the opportunities for using written evidence, and in the same year the Winn Committee on personal injuries litigation recommended that expert medical evidence should be given in written form unless it was absolutely necessary to call the doctor as a witness. They also thought it should be made compulsory to exchange medical reports. In 1969 the Payne Report on debt enforcement advocated that debtors should fill in a written questionnaire instead of undergoing oral questions on their means as at present. This would save personal attendance and be cheap and quick. The Criminal Justice Act 1967 allows written statements by witnesses to be put in evidence in committal proceedings provided no objection is made. This did not prevent the longest committal proceedings on record taking place in 1968–69. The case was that of John Bloom, the washing machine tycoon. After proceedings lasting 115 days and costing £150,000 he was committed for trial, all the evidence having to be gone through again at even greater length. The degree to which oral evidence can safely be dispensed with is obviously limited. Apart from the value of cross-examination, written evidence does not necessarily save time. This was shown by the old practice of the ecclesiastical courts in England, which gave rise to scandalous delays only ended when the law was changed to permit the taking of oral evidence in court and the ending of the system whereby the testimony of witnesses was reduced to writing beforehand by an examiner sitting in private.

It should be simpler to require *argument* to be submitted in writing, since cross-examination is not involved. Admittedly the parallel of the United States Supreme Court, where written 'briefs' are submitted to the court in advance, is not encouraging. Counsel are reluctant to leave out any point which may conceivably help them, and the briefs are often very prolix. The time of judges is not saved, and oral argument on the brief is common. The judges in England, however, can be relied on to castigate unnecessary prolixity, and the Bar would respond. English lawyers are well aware that adding weak arguments to strong ones lessens persuasiveness.

Can we go further and envisage civil proceedings that are entirely in written form and dispense altogether with a hearing? In appellate courts which do not hear evidence this is obviously possible. In arbitration proceedings, and before some administrative tribunals, written material alone is used. In a case decided in 1915 the Local Government Board decided an appeal against an order closing a dwelling-house merely on the written report of the inspector concerned, who had heard the appellant's arguments. The appellant's contention that the Board should have allowed him to appear before them failed to convince the House of Lords. The judgment of Lord Justice Hamilton in the Court of Appeal contained the following significant passage:

> It is said that a written argument is an illusory thing, that there is no eloquence or at least no persuasion but in speech. . . . I find the contention bewildering. Are reasoning and writing mutually exclusive processes? The appellant desires to enjoy what Mr. Upjohn felicitously calls 'the bound and rebound of ideas and arguments between the Bench and the Bar.' This invests with authority a practice (or should I say a foible?) of judges, which I had believed to be pardonable and hoped to be not without its uses, but I am unable to see that it is the very pith of the administration of natural justice.

This is clear sanction for doing justice by documentary means. It may not be the best justice possible, but it is far better than no justice at all. To return to Lord Devlin: 'Time and money must be decisive considerations if delay and prohibitive cost prevent (as they unquestionably do) the object of justice itself from being attained. In order that a few might have a whole loaf of bread baked to perfection, the great majority starve. . . . If by slightly increasing the margin of error, the percentage of cost can be reduced it is only the idealist who will revolt.' One point needs to be stressed. The use of written material should not be allowed to lessen the public nature of the administration of justice. It follows that copies of all documents considered by the court should be available for public inspection.

COST LIMITS

More stringent methods may be needed to reduce costs effectively, or at least to ensure that they bear some relation to the subject matter. It is hardly right to place the judicial resources of the state at the unlimited disposal of litigants who have lost all sense of proportion, like those who once disputed before Lord Justice Knight Bruce over a sum of £10 odd. Their squabble brought from him these memorable words:

> . . . upon a matter that, if they had not good sense enough to settle it for themselves some respectable neighbour would probably upon application have adjusted for them in an hour–began (as I collect), the career of cost, and heat, and hatred, of reproach, scandal and misery, in which they are now engaged, of which neither this day nor this year nor perhaps another will, I fear, see the end, and which seems well to exemplify an old English saying, that the mother of mischief is no bigger than a midge's wing.

The Evershed Committee in 1953 considered suggestions for restricting costs chargeable or recoverable and rejected them in the belief that their modest proposals for procedural reform would make such expedients unnecessary. This has not proved the case, and the time is ripe for looking at the matter again. By analogy with the statutory limitation on candidates' expenses at elections, it should be possible to devise a system under which a claim for a specific sum could not be pursued at a total cost exceeding say half that sum. Professional fees in excess would not be recoverable; unsuccessful defendants would be limited in the costs they had to bear. Where the claim was not quantified cost limitation would be more difficult, but still possible by preliminary decision of a master or registrar. This might be rough justice, only achieved perhaps by dispensing with an oral hearing altogether. It would be better than no justice at all, even if it came down to parties in a trivial dispute telling their story in person to the judge and abiding by his immediate decision without right of appeal. The law could do with less formality, but that is matter for another chapter.

5

Dais, Dock and Fancy Dress

To the lay observer, proceedings in the High Court of Justice resemble a cross between a theatrical performance and the celebration of High Mass. Perched on the altar, as it were, and receiving corresponding reverence, is the judge clothed in colourful robes and a horsehair wig. Immediately beneath him, at a very much lower level, sits the associate or clerk of the court, also wearing a wig but in a black gown. Counsel similarly attired address the judge from the front row of the stalls (if their gown is of silk) or the second row (if of stuff). On the prompt side of the proscenium is placed the jury box, while on the O.P. side is the witness stand, resembling a pulpit. The audience or congregation are ranged in the stalls and gallery, and the press are in attendance for what is invariably the first and only performance (though it may be repeated on appeal). The usher, like a sort of verger, stands in his own type of black gown with testament in hand ready to administer the oath to the actors in the drama, the witnesses. The play may be comedy, tragedy or burlesque; often it partakes of all three. Sometimes it goes on tour, when the judge makes his circuit of the Assize towns. Then it takes on the air of a pageant. In the Criminal Courts things are much the same, with the addition of one further piece of stage equipment–the dock. Derived from the Flemish docke, a birdcage, this is a place of ignominy in which accused persons (although presumed innocent since not yet proved guilty) are installed while their fate is decided. With true legal impartiality the seats provided for everyone (except the judge) are of a uniform hardness. Discomfort it seems is treated, as with church pews, as an aid to salvation. Or perhaps it is tolerated because admission, as to a church, is free though the parties involved will pay dearly for the privilege of mounting the performance.

It will be seen therefore that along with the talkative road to truth, we have as a cherished part of our legal system the picturesque, or ceremonial, road to truth. The conservatism of lawyers has led them to retain features, which, once generally prevalent, have disappeared elsewhere except in the higher reaches of the established Church, the courts of Royalty, and the High Court of Parliament. Of nothing is this more true than legal dress.

The history of legal dress is intricate and obscure–a study in itself for those who are interested. From the close of the Middle Ages lawyers were known as 'gentlemen of the long robe' in token of their having declined to join those who in the middle of the fourteenth century reacted against the garments generally worn in favour of a short, tight tunic or surcoat. The judicial ermine has a direct descent through the centuries, though in fact it has long ceased to embody the pelt of the ermine or common stoat of northern latitudes. Newer forms of judicial costume, as those of modern creations such as County Court judges, have been modelled on dress of ancient descent. In the same way the new universities hasten to copy Oxford and Cambridge academic gowns, though with variations and more venturesome colour schemes. The lawyer's sartorial equipment is completed by eighteenth-century starched linen bands tied round a nineteenth-century starched wing-collar and, beneath the gown, a black jacket, waistcoat and striped trousers belonging perhaps to the earlier twentieth century. Judges, immune from observation below the head and shoulders themselves (except when in motion), have often reacted strongly to irregularities of dress among members of the Bar. Mr Justice Byles objected to the appearance of Lord Coleridge as a young barrister because his legs were 'encased in light grey trousers'. Another judge pointedly looked through a young counsel who rose to address him, and remained oblivious to his arguments. Finally he said, 'I can't see you Mr So-and-so' and the young man was forced to resume his seat. It later transpired that he had a waistcoat button undone.

Most distinctive of all is the legal wig, which has not survived anywhere else except in Parliament–though that is scarcely an exception since it has many of the attributes of a Court of Law. Wigs lack the ancient origin of robes. They first became generally fashionable in the Court of Louis XIV. When originally donned by young barristers in England, they were regarded rather as long hair and sideburns are today by the more staid. Many judges thought them 'coxcombical' and refused to allow barristers to appear in their courts when so attired. The long curled periwig in fashion during the Restoration period was discarded by barristers, in common with other gentlemen of quality, in the first quarter of the eighteenth century in favour of the more convenient short, curled model. The full-bottomed wig continued to be worn by judges and Queen's counsel, as it is today on formal occasions. The barrister's wig in its final form has been described as a combination of the tye wig and the Ramillies peruke. The tye wig worn by judges today differs from the barrister's wig only in having one curl instead of two – a vertical one just over the tail of the wig. Like the barrister's wig the judicial wig came into vogue in the late seventeenth and early eighteenth century. As late as the time of Sir John Powel, a Queen's Bench judge who died in 1713, it was not invariably worn. His statue in the Lady Chapel of Gloucester Cathedral shows him in skull cap but no wig.

The effect of donning the elaborate legal costume is to induce a temporary change of character. A layman who dresses up in this way for a performance of *Trial by Jury* feels he has entered an artificial world, and taken a step back into the past. The effect on lawyers is hardly different. Though they become accustomed to their costume it still removes them from everyday life and emphasises that they are now part of a different world, where people are more ceremonious, more deliberate, and more disposed to behave as people behaved in the past, when society was hierarchical and technology had not been thought of. Thus deference to the judge, and courtesy to one's opponent, come naturally. Counsel lards his speech with antique phrases like 'may it please your lordship' and 'if I may submit, with the greatest respect . . .' The court, until reminded otherwise, still treats the witnesses as part of a Christian society and expects them to give their evidence upon oath. If their religion requires the oath to be administered in a peculiar way, this will be done. Thus Jews may swear with their hats on, Scotsmen with uplifted hand, and Buddhists by breaking a saucer. There is one religion which requires oaths to be administered by spilling the blood of a cockerel with its throat newly slit, but this has not given any noticeable trouble to the High Court of Justice. Encouraged by the judge, such eccentric oath-takers may instead affirm–a procedure which has been available since the Oaths Act of 1888. This Act includes the typically British provision that if an oath has been duly taken the fact that the person taking it had no religious belief does not affect its validity. The Act was a notable departure for a society which valued meticulous observance of formalities, and which privately censured one judge, Baron Bramwell, because he did not insist upon a witness removing his glove whilst taking the oath and because, in passing judgment upon a man convicted of a hideous murder, he omitted the usual prayer that God might have mercy on his soul. 'My duty is to pass upon you the sentence of death for that offence, and that is my only duty', he remarked with refreshing lack of humbug.

CONTEMPT OF COURT

A system using the methods we have described is inevitably standing on its dignity. Rules exist to protect this. There have been numerous examples of disappointed litigants giving vent to their displeasure in the face of the court. One seventeenth-century instance was reported in the vile mixture of English, French and Latin then employed. The report relates how the prisoner was annoyed at his treatment by the judge and thereupon 'ject un Brickbat a le dit Justice que narrowly mist, & pur ceo immediately fuit Indictment drawn per noy envers le prisoner, & son dexter manus ampute & fix al gibbet sur que luy mesme immediatement hang in presence de Court'. Modern litigants throw fruit rather than brickbats. In 1913, when a suffragette leader was sentenced to prison in a Scottish court, her sympathisers discharged a fusillade of apples at the judge, while in 1938 the judges of the Court of Appeal in London had to take refuge from a barrage of tomatoes. Such conduct as this constitutes contempt of court, and is the only crime which can be tried summarily in the Superior Court. The court has an immediate power to commit the offender to prison until he has purged his contempt by suitable apology. A fine may also be imposed, and the court is not limited in the amount of this.

Contempt in the face of the court includes any action which tends to interfere with the course of justice. Apart from physical attack on jury, counsel or witnesses, this would include threatening language and any other conduct likely to disturb the even course of judicial proceedings. The crime of contempt goes much wider than acts in the precincts of the court itself however. Anything done before the trial which may prejudice its proper conduct is punishable. Indeed actions following the trial may be punishable if they might tend to deter others from proper participation in future judicial proceedings. The brother of a convicted man was himself convicted for contempt over his conduct to the foreman of the jury. He had challenged him to mortal combat for having bullied the jury into convicting his brother. The judge said that jurors must be protected from all interference with them in the discharge of their duties, from all attempt to assail their characters or reputations, and from the imputation of motives other than those which should actuate men having such solemn and important duties to discharge.

Most contempt cases, however, relate to the conduct of newspapers. The desire to present their readers with up-to-the minute news is sometimes difficult to reconcile with the need to avoid premature disclosure of facts or arguments which might prejudice the fair trial of an accused. From the moment a person is arrested he is under the protection of the Court in this respect, and the most innocent reporting of his alleged crime may land the newspaper in trouble. In 1936 for example a man was charged with unlawful possession of firearms as the result of an incident during a royal procession. A newsreel film of his arrest was shown with the caption 'Attempt on the King's Life'. This clearly implied that the arrested man was guilty of an offence, and the distributors of the film were fined £50 for contempt of court. Other cases are less straightforward. It has been held contempt to publish photographs, however innocently, which might influence the recollection or evidence of witnesses likely to be called at the trial. It has even been suggested, in the 1968 case concerning the ingenious financier Dr Savundra, that contempt may be committed before any proceedings have begun if there is reason to believe they are imminent. This concerned a television interview with Savundra, and Lord Justice Salmon remarked that 'trial by television is not to be tolerated in a civilised society'. Nor does liability for contempt cease with the conviction of the accused. If he has not yet been sentenced, any published comment which might influence the sentence will be contempt. Even after sentence it is contempt to publish comments which could influence the result of an appeal. Admittedly, since questions of appeal are in the hands of judges rather than lay jurors, they are less likely to be influenced and the law will not punish comments unless they are strong. As Lord Chief Justice Parker remarked, a judge is in no sense superhuman but he has by his training no difficulty in putting out of his mind matters which are not evidence in the case.

It was for pointing out in some detail that the late Mr Justice Darling was not superhuman that the editor of a local newspaper once got into trouble. But then he expressed himself in somewhat extreme language:

> If anyone can imagine Little Tich upholding his dignity upon a point of honour in a public house, he has a very fair conception of what Mr. Justice Darling looked like in warning the Press against the printing of indecent evidence. His diminutive Lordship positively glowed with judicial self-consciousness. . . . No newspaper can exist except upon its merits, a condition from which the bench, happily for Mr. Justice Darling, is exempt. There is not a journalist in Birmingham who has anything to learn from the impudent little man in horsehair, a microcosm of conceit and empty-headedness . . . one is almost sorry that the Lord Chancellor had not another relative to provide for on the day that he selected a new judge from among the larrikins of the law. One of Mr Justice Darling's biographers states that an

> 'eccentric relative left him much money'. That misguided testator spoiled a successful bus conductor. . . .

We are less forthright today, and perhaps this is why Lord Denning felt able to say in a recent case concerning an article in *Punch* by Mr Quintin Hogg which criticised the Court of Appeal: 'we will never use this jurisdiction [i.e. to punish contempt of court] as a means to uphold our own dignity'. This is all very well while that dignity is not seriously threatened. When it is, the Court can act in no other way–unless judicial dignity itself is to go out of fashion.

THE MERITS OF DRESSING-UP

1 It would be idle to deny that there are substantial advantages in ceremonial usage. For one thing there is a practical value in dressing people with special functions in distinctive dress. This is seen in its most obvious form in Parliamentary proceedings. A Member of Parliament going about his business needs to be able readily to distinguish functionaries of the House from his fellow Members. He can identify the Speaker by his full-bottomed wig and elaborate black silk gown. The Clerk of the House or his assistant is known by his short wig and more modest gown. The Serjeant-at-Arms, who is responsible for maintaining order in the Chamber, again has a distinctive dress of tail-coat, knee-breeches and sword. Messengers wear full evening dress with white tie and a large gold badge on their chests. Policemen are dressed, helmets and all, as though on point duty. The ordinary courts use distinctive dress in a similar way. Many of these costumes are archaic, but their defenders say it would serve little purpose to abolish them, since they would merely have to be replaced by modern inventions. Furthermore they have a levelling effect and, in toning down the individuality of particular office-holders assist the impression that justice is dispensed with an even hand by officers of equal ability.

These practical considerations are not, however, the real essence of the matter. This concerns the majesty and dignity of the law. It is felt by most of us that legal proceedings should not be carried on in an atmosphere of slap-dash frivolity–though we might not go as far as Mr Justice Stephen, who used to punish unseemly laughter in his court by making the offender stand by the prisoner in the dock until the case was over. The rule of law is a cherished principle of our constitution. Respect for the law is vital to our way of life, though it needs more than archaic costumes and ceremonies to ensure its existence.

THE OTHER SIDE OF THE ARGUMENT

Despite the force of the arguments just described there is ground for saying that in our present age respect for the law is no longer enhanced by spectacle and ceremonial. *Punch*, as ever a true mirror of its time, made the point when purporting to sympathise with a judge who railed against pop guitarists making fortunes that 'put the Bar in the shade'. The crudeness of the comment does not alter its force: 'Galling to realise that there are other people, not particularly talented and affecting grotesque gear, who get fat on the knack of plugging other folks' ideas in a way that impresses an audience of dimwits.' The truth is that ceremonial has ceased to impress, though it may amuse and distract. The Duke of Windsor underlined this when revealing that he was horrified at the 'preposterous rig' he had to wear for his Investiture as Prince of Wales in 1911. Expressing the hope, partially justified, that his great-nephew's costume would be simpler at *his* Investiture, the Duke remarked that many outmoded rituals, much red carpet and paraphernalia connected with Royalty were on their way into limbo. This was, he thought, a matter of simple common sense.

There is no longer respect for antique forms and costumes, and universal education has removed much of the dread once inspired by judicial figures. The majesty of the law still deters a witness from lying, but there has been no research into the question of how far this is due to the characteristics we are discussing. What we do know is that judges are sometimes embarrassed by being set apart in peculiar dress, and try to mitigate its effect. So Mr Justice Blain recently took off his wig in court before sentencing a young mother for infanticide. He said: 'I have taken my wig off because I want you to realise we don't just deal with criminals and punish them, but also deal with people who have problems. I am trying to treat you as one of those people.' The intended meaning of these words is not altogether clear; the judge's discomfiture is. When faced with a poor creature who had done away with her newborn baby in extreme agony of mind, he clearly felt that his judicial costume was a grotesque irrelevance.

To be dressed in fine, impressive clothes and set high above everyone else is not good for weaker natures. The barrister who, having accepted a judgeship, feels that he has now, in the unkind phrase, got his bottom on the Consolidated Fund and can spend the rest of his working days sitting in judgment over his fellow men may be rare but he is by no means unknown. The right judicial attitude was shown by Mr Justice Willes: 'I take leave to say that I am not conscious of the vulgar desire to elevate myself or the court of which I may be a member, by grasping after a pre-eminence which does not belong to me.' Less noble natures too easily take in a personal way the respect accorded to them as embodiments of the Queen's justice. They regard their own convenience as the only thing that matters, and easily forget the true costs and hardships of justice inefficiently administered. Few judges today display the concern for litigants' time felt by Mr Justice Grantham at the beginning of this century. On one occasion while on circuit he was taken ill and was absolutely forbidden by his doctor to attend court. In order that time might not be wasted he sent for the Grand Jury and delivered his charge to them in his bedroom. As soon as it was possible he was taken to the court, where he sat wrapped in wadding and surrounded by old-fashioned railway-carriage footwarmers, such was his anxiety not to keep the parties and witnesses waiting.

Also to be counted as part of the cost of a ceremonial system of justice is the time taken to put on and take off elaborate costumes and wigs, and the expense of providing and maintaining them. A High Court judge will spend at least half an hour a day, if not more, merely putting on and taking off his judicial rig. The cost of providing it in new condition is over £200. Can this expense of time and money be justified in modern conditions?

Finally we may question the wisdom of making everyone in court, except the judge, physically uncomfortable. Professor Ely Devons has recorded how he suffered from the conditions in the jury box:

> . . . The Englishman must have been of much smaller bulk when the jury box was first designed, for we were miserably cramped and had to sit bolt upright for long periods; perhaps it was an astute move to make us so uncomfortable that when we did retire to the jury room we would be so weary that we would make our decision quickly.

In the days of the great defending advocate Marshall Hall it used to be a familiar sight to see his clerk bringing before him into court, along with his other impedimenta, an air-cushion which would be solemnly inflated and arranged to the great man's satisfaction before the case could begin. Conditions are the same today, except in the few newly-built courtrooms where some attempt is made to provide reasonable standards of comfort for all involved in a court case.

TOWARDS A SIMPLER PROCEDURE

It may be concluded that, while there are some virtues in a ceremonial system, it has little place in the administration of justice towards the end of the twentieth century. People are no longer impressed by fine clothes, and tend to be irritated rather than over-awed when people they think no better than themselves are given elevated status. While recently-built courtrooms may be more comfortable, they show no disposition to depart from the tradition of placing the judge in elevation, or the accused in the dock. Yet in the highest tribunals in the land – the House of Lords and the Judicial Committee of the Privy Council – the simplest arrangements are followed. The law lords do not wear wigs and robes. Dressed in ordinary lounge suits, they listen to the arguments addressed to them while sitting on the same level as the advocates. The same applies in most other countries, and there is little doubt that in time English courts will follow suit. Lawyers would do well to ensure that these inevitable changes come as early as possible, rather than being deferred until public opinion insists upon them. The legal profession is not so popular with the public that it can afford to stand upon its dignity rather than accepting equality with the ordinary citizen.

Some reformers have urged the abolition of oath-taking. Mr David Napley argues that since religion is such a recognised basis for prejudice that it is eschewed in social conversation it ought also to be excluded from our courts of law. 'There can be few persons competent to give evidence', he adds, 'who do not realise it is their duty, to the best of their recollection and ability, to give a true account of fact, and fewer, if any, who do not know that deliberately to give false evidence can lead to a charge of perjury.' Mr Napley appears to advocate even giving up affirmation as part of court procedure. It is desirable to retain some way of reminding a witness of his duty to tell the truth–perhaps by a formula stating the penalties for perjury. While even a proportion of the population retain religious belief, however, it seems of doubtful wisdom to drop the oath which for them at least must increase the likelihood of truthful testimony.

Finally it is convenient to note here that reform of the law of contempt of court, so as to bring it more in line with public notions of justice, took place in 1960. The previous law operated harshly against persons who were free from moral blame, and the new Act provides a defence for a person who, having distributed offending matter, can prove that he did not know, and had no reason to suspect, that it was present. For the first time the Act provided a right of appeal to persons convicted of contempt of court, thus reducing the arbitrary power of the judges. That further reforms in the law of contempt may still be needed is shown by the 1968 prosecution of those responsible for a *Sunday Times* article about one Malik who was awaiting trial under the Race Relations Act. The paper described him as having had 'an unedifying career as a brothel keeper, procurer and property racketeer'. While this was clearly prejudicial, the editor and proprietors did not personally know of it. Furthermore they had devised a scheme which the court found to be an elaborate and reasonable system to avoid contempt of court. Nevertheless the paper was fined the large sum of £5,000, and one commentator remarked that this revealed a defect in the 1960 Act. Another matter that needs attention is the fact that even where a case of contempt is brought against those directly responsible for commenting on pending litigation it is far from certain what type of comment merits censure and what is the extent of the quarantine period during which no prejudicial matter is tolerated. These are vital matters concerning freedom of speech itself. Both the court and the public must be constantly on the alert to keep restrictive rules down to the minimum required for the protection of accused persons. To withdraw matters of public concern from public comment is intolerable where it is not absolutely necessary.

Happily, no further reforms seem needed in the law of contempt of court so far as it relates to upholding the dignified ceremonial of the courts. What is wanted is for that ceremonial to be modified so as to remove archaic features from those courts where they still remain.

6

Legal Aid

Critics of the law used to say that the courts were open to all–like the Ritz Hotel. Certainly no one involved in legal proceedings has ever been prevented from handling his case himself through all its stages. Even today, with legal aid freely available to those of inadequate means, the litigant in person is by no means a rarity. The layman seeking to grapple by himself with the intricacies of court procedure has a severe task. Judges do everything in their power, however, to see that justice is done. From this it might be thought that no injustice would result if those who could not afford legal assistance were left to present their own case. It is worth spending a little time inquiring why this is not so.

We have seen that the adversary system of English justice places the judge in the position of an umpire or arbiter between two contestants. For the system to work properly the contestants must be evenly matched and equally familiar with legal principles and procedure. The inquisitorial system of the Continent, which gives the presiding judge or magistrate an active role in ferreting out the truth, makes the position of unrepresented parties less difficult. There is much more to it than this, however.

The ordinary man or woman with a story to tell and a case to make wants to do it right away and is impatient of artificial restrictions. If he is the defendant, however, his first utterance to the court will not be (as he probably expects) an explanation of his own case; it will be the cross-examination of his opponent's witnesses. When his turn comes to cross-examine the first witness he will probably start with a series of statements instead of questions, will tend to assume that the witness knows all about his case, and will often ask questions the answers to which damage rather than assist his cause. When he comes to give evidence himself he will find that the rules of evidence prevent him telling his story in the most natural way. At all points he will be pulled up by the judge for breaking rules of whose existence he is totally unaware. He is likely to become more and more flustered, and the judge to become more and more irritated.

These difficulties are exacerbated if the litigant in person lacks, as will often be the case, the educational and cultural advantages of the judge and other lawyers he encounters in court, or if he lacks experience of expressing himself and constructing rational arguments. The difficulties of class and background are illustrated by the story of the workman who gave evidence that an incident had occurred 'during the dinner hour'. The judge asked if he could not be more precise, 'since the dinner hour may be anything from 7 to 9'.

To these difficulties there are of course added the hazards arising from ignorance of the law. Although judges and opposing Counsel will draw attention to legal points of assistance to the litigant, this is no substitute for the full preparation of a legal argument and the taking of points as they arise in the course of proceedings. While the need for representation by a professional advocate might be reduced if court procedures were simplified, the difficulty posed by ignorance of the law appears insurmountable.

Naturally the importance of being represented in court depends on the consequences likely to flow from losing the case. These are obviously most serious in criminal cases involving a risk of imprisonment, loss of employment or social disgrace. By a decision of the United States Supreme Court in 1962 no person may now be tried for a criminal offence in a Federal or State Court unless he is legally represented or has waived the right to be represented. At about the same time the Lord Chief Justice of England expressed the view that in almost every case of the trial of an indictable offence the interests of the accused could only be safeguarded by legal representation. Apart from the work of the advocate in court, the preparation of a case of any complexity can only with difficulty be carried out without the facilities and experience available in a solicitor's office. This especially applies to the tracing and interviewing of witnesses. The obtaining of expert evidence, and the cross-examination of expert witnesses also calls for specialised techniques.

The legal aid system established in 1949 provides adequately for litigants and accused persons of small means, but not so well for those with slightly greater resources. The system applies to both civil and criminal proceedings, though with some differences and some exceptions. The legal aid service is under the general control of the Lord Chancellor, and is administered by the Law Society.

In general there are three situations in which legal aid may be sought. An applicant may wish to assert or dispute a claim at a stage when there is not yet any question of litigation, or he may want to bring or defend a case in the courts, or he may want to appeal or defend an appeal. To obtain legal aid in a civil case, the applicant must satisfy the local Legal Aid Committee (composed of lawyers) that there are good grounds for bringing or defending the proceedings and that his means are within the prescribed limit. Legal Aid is free for an applicant whose disposable income is under £250 per annum and whose disposable capital does not exceed £125. Above these limits, but below the upper limit, a successful applicant must make some contribution towards the costs. This upper limit is a disposable income of £700 and disposable capital of about £500. Certain necessary payments and assets are deducted in arriving at disposable income or capital. These include rent, rates and taxes.

Similar provisions apply to criminal cases, though a somewhat different test of whether legal aid is justified is applied, and the decision is made by the court and not the Legal Aid Committee. In a criminal case there is no question of whether the proceedings should be brought; the accused is a party to the proceedings whether he likes it or not and has no option to withdraw. The question is not 'has he a good case?' but 'do the interests of justice require that he should be represented?' At Assizes and Quarter-Sessions, where the more serious criminal cases are tried, more than two-thirds of prisoners pleading not guilty are represented by counsel or solicitor under the legal aid system. Research by the

Widgery Committee showed only 7 per cent of prisoners having no legal representation at all.

By far the greatest number of criminal prosecutions are tried in Magistrates' Courts by summary procedure. The number of cases so dealt with in each year is approximately 1,500,000, ranging in seriousness from shopbreaking and malicious wounding to chimney fires and failure to obtain a dog licence. The Widgery Committee found a general measure of agreement that legal aid should rarely be necessary for the great majority of summary offences. The proportion of cases in which it is actually granted is less than two per cent. This figure is put into perspective by the fact that applications to magistrates for legal aid are granted in over three-quarters of the cases where they are made.

CRITICISMS OF CIVIL AID SYSTEM

In the past twenty years very great improvements have been made in ensuring that people who cannot afford normal legal representation in the courts are not forced to conduct their own proceedings or let the matter go by default. For several centuries a poor person could only obtain legal assistance if he sued *in forma pauperis* ('in the character of a pauper'). He had to swear that he had not property worth £5, except his clothing and the subject matter of his action. He was then allowed to bring his action without payment of court fees and to have assigned to him a solicitor and counsel who acted without payment. This procedure was not finally brought to an end until 1949. The parallel in criminal cases, the 'dock brief' lingered until the Criminal Justice Act 1967 gave statutory effect to the main recommendations of the Widgery Committee. Yet despite improvements, there are still a number of points on which reforms are advocated. We look first at civil proceedings.

The points of criticism are naturally enough those where limits are applied to the aid scheme. It does not operate in certain types of proceedings, or where certain causes of action are involved, or of course where a party's financial resources (though perhaps not large) exceed the prescribed limits. Legal aid is available in all the ordinary civil courts; the question of its extension to other forms of proceedings, such as those before the Lands Tribunal, Insurance Tribunals, and Rent Assessment Tribunals, is considered in Chapter 10 since it is bound up with the much simpler procedure operating in such tribunals.

When the present system of legal aid was introduced in 1949 it was applied to all civil causes of action except defamation (libel and slander), breach of promise of marriage, loss of services of a woman or girl in consequence of her rape or seduction, and enticement of spouses. It was argued that to give aid for such proceedings would be to risk abuse and the waste of public money. This has been a source of controversy ever since. It is logical to argue, as some have done, that if the law gives legal remedies in such cases there is no justification for withholding the necessary financial aid to pursue the remedies. The latest view of the Lord Chancellor's advisory committee on the subject is that the exclusion in the case of defamation (the only important one) should continue. The reasoning is curious. It is said that actions, specially for slander, are likely to be brought against defendants of the same background as the plaintiff. If the plaintiff is impecunious so therefore would the defendant be, and the result would be legal aid on both sides with no funds out of which any damages awarded could be paid. To the argument that defendants in libel cases are often newspaper proprietors commanding large resources, the committee weakly reply that such an action should be capable of settlement at an early stage by an apology, payment of costs and a reasonable sum in compensation. If all defendants were as reasonable as this there would be no need for the legal aid scheme at all! The committee is, however, prepared to support the removal of one curious feature arising from the exclusion of defamation actions. The exclusion relates to actions 'wholly *or partly*' in respect of defamation. This means that a legally aided plaintiff alleging a cause of action having nothing to do with defamation could lose his legal aid if the defendant counter-claimed for damages for libel or slander. Cases very occasionally occur where legal aid is given to a plaintiff claiming damages for wrongful dismissal from his employment.

If, as is likely, words have been exchanged between the parties at the time of the incident it is a simple matter for the employer to counter-claim for damages for slander. This effectively brings the case to an end because the dismissed employee, deprived of legal aid, cannot continue the action.

The argument that the income limits for legal aid are too low and should be revised has much force. A person whose disposable income is several times that at present allowed could still suffer severely from having to meet all the costs of himself and his opponent in an unsuccessful action. Lord Chancellor Gardiner has accepted the case for revising the financial limit 'when economic conditions allow'. One commentator has cogently argued that there should be no limits at all, since the bigger an applicant's income or capital the more he is required to contribute to the costs. It is pointed out that to a man of comfortable means the advantage of being legally aided would not lie in receiving help towards meeting the costs of bringing or defending the action but in being covered against the costs of appeal. It is possible in rare cases for an action begun in the County Court to go on appeal first to the Court of Appeal and then the House of Lords. Costs which were quite modest in the first instance can thus become inflated to an amount which could cripple even a comparatively wealthy man.

The legal aid system is mainly used for divorce and other matrimonial proceedings, and domestic proceedings in Magistrates' Courts. These account for about 80 per cent of the total cost to the taxpayer of legal aid for civil cases. This total may be reduced by the recent decision to allow County Courts to try matrimonial causes. Nevertheless it remains true that far more is spent by the state on enabling people to terminate their marriages than is spent on marriage counselling to help preserve them.

A serious objection to the working of the legal aid scheme arose where one party to proceedings was legally aided while the other, having greater financial resources, was ineligible for aid. Particularly unjust was the case where a person of fairly modest means was sued by a legally aided plaintiff, successfully resisted the claim, and was awarded costs, which he was never able to recover. He could not recover them from the plaintiff because he had no money, and he could not recover them from the legal aid fund (which had financed the plaintiff's litigation) because the law did not permit. An Act was passed in 1964 to deal with this injustice. The court was empowered to order costs to be paid out of the legal aid fund, but only where four conditions were satisfied. The proceedings must have been started by the person receiving legal aid, the court must be satisfied that in all circumstances it was just and equitable to meet the costs out of public funds, and that the unassisted party would suffer 'severe financial hardship' unless an order was made, and must consider how far if at all the other party could be made to pay. Though hailed as a measure of reform this Act has proved to be largely a dead letter. The Law Society retained £48,000 in the first year to meet claims expected to be made under the Act; in fact the total awarded was £160. The conditions proved too stringent, the courts too reluctant to grant relief, and the scope of the relief inadequate. There is also no justification for depriving an unassisted *plaintiff* of his costs from the legal aid fund where it is only the existence of that fund which enabled the defendant to wage his unsuccessful defence. Without it he might well have been obliged to settle the plaintiff's claim on terms ultimately far more advantageous.

Another point on which reforms are sought concerns the rule which requires those administering the legal aid fund to recoup subsidies to a successful plaintiff out of damages awarded to him. This seems a reasonable rule, but in practice it works badly. The interests of justice require that wherever possible contested actions should be settled either before they reach trial or any rate before the end of the proceedings. An assisted plaintiff who might otherwise accept an offer from the other side of a payment in settlement of his claim is often reluctant to do so where the amount paid would largely go to the legal aid fund. If a waiver or reduction of the claim of the fund were permitted more actions could be settled, and ultimately the fund would benefit through the saving of costs incurred in fighting the case to its end.

NEW SCHEME OF CRIMINAL AID

Until the new scheme of criminal aid, introduced in 1967, the granting of aid was an all or nothing affair. Either the accused's costs were met in full or he was given no assistance. This defect has now been removed, and criminal aid brought into line with the civil system. Although the decision whether to grant aid is made by the court before or at the beginning of the trial, the assessment of the contribution (if any) which the accused is to make to the costs of his defence is deferred until the end. This is because until the outcome of the trial is known it may be very difficult to assess the financial position of the accused. If he is found guilty and sent to prison he will probably be unable to make any financial contribution at all, whereas if he is acquitted or merely fined his earning capacity may be unimpaired. Also introduced are new provisions directed to enabling checks to be made on the financial circumstances of applicants for aid. Formerly the court had little to go on except the unsupported word of the accused as to his financial resources. Now it is empowered to call for help in investigating his finances from the Supplementary Benefits Commission (formerly the National Assistance Board).

The new Act has been criticised on the ground that defendants are likely to forego legal aid if forced to meet some part of the cost, particularly since the amount that will have to be met cannot be known until the proceedings are over. It is said that a high proportion of defendants are unwilling to spend their own money on lawyers. The figures given by the Widgery Committee itself showed that of accused persons refused legal aid on the ground that their means were thought to be sufficient to pay for their own legal assistance, only one-third in fact did so. This criticism has some force. The new system compels an accused, in unfavourable circumstances, to gamble on whether the benefits likely to flow from the services of solicitor and counsel will or will not outweigh the problematical amount that, at the end of the day, the court may order him to bear. Only experience of the working of the Act can demonstrate whether these criticisms are sufficient to warrant a return to the previous system, or at least the fixing of the maximum contribution at the outset.

ALTERNATIVES TO LEGAL AID

Those, and they seem to be a growing number, who favour the setting up of comprehensive state systems for every social purpose would like to see the legal aid system replaced by a State legal service. It is true that, as we saw in Chapter 3, the Society of Labour Lawyers would only have their proposed local legal centres dealing with litigation in exceptional cases. If the centres were established, however, there is no doubt that within a short time pressure would come for their expansion.

On the criminal side, criticisms are levelled at defects in the legal aid system arising from its dependence on the assignment of counsel and solicitors in ordinary practice. This means that, as the Widgery Committee found, the proper standard is not invariably reached. A minority of solicitors fail to display the same standards in legal aid cases as they do in private practice. They neglect to prepare their cases adequately and do not interview their client until he is brought to the court. Prison governors testify to mental stress suffered by some prisoners when their solicitors fail to visit them, or send along youthful untrained clerks. The Law Society frowns on such neglect, and endeavours to stamp it out.

Some reformers put forward as an alternative to the legal aid system in criminal cases the establishment of public defenders, who would be employed by the state and do nothing else but defend poor prisoners. Three attempts were made by Horatio Bottomley, himself a noted litigant in person, to persuade Parliament to set up an office of Public Defender in the early 1920s but without success. The system is in operation in some states of America, notably California and Illinois. Congress has, however, rejected the use of this institution in Federal criminal courts.

A proposal to introduce the Public Defender in Canada was rejected after a special committee had examined the working of the system in the United States. This committee found that the chief advantage of a Public Defender system was its cheapness, but that it had many drawbacks. It was wrong in principle since both prosecution and defender were employed by the same master and the adversary system was impaired. Defences tended to become perfunctory and impersonal; there was little incentive to counsel to exert his best efforts. It had the appearance of charity, and was inevitably regarded as a second-rate alternative available only to the poor. One of the most serious objections found by the committee was the effect on the criminal Bar. Where the defence of accused persons is concentrated so heavily in a few hands the inevitable result is a shrinkage of the independent criminal Bar.

The Widgery Committee in England found similar objections. While Public Defenders would become specialists this would be more than offset by depriving accused persons of the right of choosing their own legal representative. Prisoners would be unlikely to have any confidence in public officials who would probably be regarded as part of the establishment.

Few people, whatever their financial circumstances, can be expected to enjoy becoming involved in litigation or criminal proceedings. Only a rich man (or a penniless one) can be sure of emerging from them without financial hardship. The question how far the state should go in meeting this must always be a difficult one, decided not on clear principles but by balancing available resources with the extent of need. One small improvement ought to be made, if only on principle. Legal aid is not available to the prosecutor in criminal proceedings. Normally this does not matter, because the prosecution is conducted by public officials – either the police or the Director of Public Prosecutions. The law does, however, make provision for private prosecutions. Department stores and large shops often bring private prosecutions against shoplifters; no question of legal aid for the prosecutor arises here. In another class of case, however, it does. This is where a sense of grievance is felt, as over an assault between neighbours or members of a family, and the police refuse to prosecute. The result may be proceedings in a magistrates' court between parties who are in the same position financially, but only one of whom (the defendant) can get legal aid. The right to bring private prosecutions is an important safeguard of liberty, since otherwise the question of whether to prosecute would be entirely in the hands of public authorities. This safeguard should not be weakened by denying its use to those with insufficient financial resources.

7

Debt and Default

DEBTS BY THE MILLION

More people tangle with the law through getting into debt than for any other reason. In England and Wales alone about one million people are sued for debt every year. Eighty-five per cent of all writs issued are for the recovery of debts. The largest group of debtors consists of married men who are weekly wage earners and have contracted multiple obligations with no resources other than their weekly earnings. A person sued for debt by one creditor is very likely to be owing many other debts at the same time. If he falls into arrears with hire-purchase instalments he is probably in arrears also with other obligations such as rent, rates, gas and electricity. Yet under the present system of enforcement each debt is dealt with by the courts individually, and each creditor can pursue his remedy without regard to the claims of others. This harms both debtor and creditor. The debtor has no sooner gone through court proceedings on one debt, terminating in an order to pay by instalments, than he is faced with further writs. Creditors are each forced to seek priority for their own debt and, as the Payne Committee put it in 1969, 'The machinery of the courts becomes a game in which the prize goes to the swiftest and sometimes to the least deserving. The game becomes a "free for all" and the reasonable or indulgent creditor may be overtaken by the demanding or exacting creditor.'

There are many judgment debtors who are never out of debt. Some become so skilled in court procedure that they can delay proceedings and cause the costs to mount up in a way which often renders enforcement of the debt uneconomic. As the TUC recognise, the extension of hire-purchase and housing mortgages has reduced the social opprobrium attached to indebtedness. The virtues of thrift and living within one's income are out of fashion, and as Lord Greene, a famous Master of the Rolls, once put it, a great deal of court time is taken up with people 'who are persuaded by persons they do not know to enter into contracts they do not understand to purchase goods they do not want with money they have not got'. The resulting problems are dealt with by a system which the Law Society has described as being a most unsatisfactory area of legal practice in which the available machinery is cumbersome, tardy, uneconomic and often ineffectual.

The creditor whose debtor will not pay faces two successive hurdles. He must first obtain a judgment from a court that the debt is owed and due for payment, and he must then enforce the judgment. In both cases he is faced by a bewildering multiplicity and choice of courts and procedures. This has grown up in a haphazard fashion over the centuries. A man who has failed to pay his way may at the same time have judgments and enforcement proceedings taken against him in the High Court, the County Court and the Magistrates' Courts. Through unconnected legal processes he may have his bank account attached by High Court order, his furniture seized by the County Court bailiff and his person committed to prison by the magistrates. In certain areas he may even be subjected to orders by such surviving antiquities as the Tolzey Court of Bristol, the Liverpool Court of Passage or the Norwich Guildhall Court of Record.

The different procedures obtaining in the various courts are illustrated by the rules regarding instalment orders. Usually the only way to get money from an insolvent or reluctant debtor is by instalments, and the machinery for this is crucial. In the County Courts the machinery has existed in reasonably satisfactory form for over a hundred years. Parliament early recognised that the small debtor was unlikely to be able to pay a judgment debt immediately but even so the machinery provided is complicated. When a County Court action is begun a form is served on the defendant enabling him to admit the claim if he so wishes, and offer to pay by instalments of whatever monthly amount is convenient to him. This is a useful procedure where there is no dispute as to liability, and it enables a hearing to be avoided. If the debtor's offer is reasonable the creditor will usually be glad to accept it and avoid further costs. The creditor is assisted in deciding whether the offer is reasonable by answers to certain questions as to his means which the debtor is obliged to give. Even where the debtor does not offer to pay by instalments in this way, the County Court can itself order him to do so and frequently does. It is remarkable that no procedure for the payment of judgment debts by instalments applies in the High Court, which in most other respects has powers exceeding those of County Courts.

Quite apart from the inconsistencies and discrepancies just mentioned, there is the further confusion caused by the existence of the quite separate and no less complicated law of bankruptcy and insolvency. Even if the procedure for the enforcement of judgment debts were rationalised its operation would still be liable to disruption at the instance of any creditor (or even the debtor himself) who wished to have the debtor's affairs dealt with under the bankruptcy machinery.

The ramshackle nature of the present system of debt enforcement often bears hardly on debtors. It is particularly bewildering and oppressive to the inadequate or unfortunate debtor genuinely struggling to free himself from burdens which, although self-imposed, are none the less onerous. The system is no less satisfactory to creditors. The Payne Committee received much evidence, 'some of it expressed in strong, even virulent, language', complaining that courts lean heavily in favour of debtors and that the present system is designed to help the debtor and not the creditor. In an attempt to defeat the inadequacies of the system, the more ruthless creditors may press forward quickly while the more considerate would prefer to give the debtor a chance to put his affairs in order.

Some creditors carry ruthlessness to the limits of legality, or even beyond. Rather than waste time in court procedure they take direct action, either themselves or by assigning the debt to professional debt-collectors. Unofficial methods of debt collection include a number of questionable tactics. There is the 'blue frightener', a notice of intention to start County Court proceedings printed on blue paper so as to resemble a County Court summons. This may be followed by the 'red frightener', which is a printed notice in red lettering headed, 'You have four days in which to reduce your debt'. If these devices fail they are likely to be followed by more concrete threats, rather than actual court proceedings. The threat to tell a man's neighbour or his employer, or to send round a van boldly painted 'Bad Debt Collection Van' can be very effective. So also can constant personal visits or telephone calls, particularly early in the morning or very late at night. More serious are actual threats of force, or personal calls accompanied by a fierce-looking dog. The Payne Committee found that some creditors were prepared to use any method and to go to unacceptable lengths to harass and intimidate debtors, instilling in them fear and panic. 'Such creditors disdain the law, which they regard as insufficient or inadequate for their purposes, and endeavour to bypass it by using strongarm tactics or cunning devices. They meet criticism of their practices by affecting moral indignation at the failure of the debtors to honour their contracts.'

DISTRESS AND EXECUTION

A form of self-help which the law expressly allows is the remedy of distress, or seizure of goods. This is one of the most ancient and barnacle-encrusted parts of the law, going back to the days when the tenants of feudal lords were obliged to render services instead of, or in addition to, rent. An abbot or prior might hold of his lord by divine service, requiring the tenant to sing a mass every Friday. If he failed in this duty the lord could seize, by the process appropriately known as distress, the furniture of the abbey or priory. Nowadays distress without any preliminary court action mainly survives as a landlords' remedy for non-payment of rent. The landlord is entitled to seize and sell whatever goods may be found on the premises let to the tenant, though some goods are excepted from seizure. A court order is unnecessary, except for dwellings within the protection of rent control. A distress cannot be made on Sunday or in the night. Where the remedy is available the tenant cannot apply for a stay of the distress or pay the amount of the arrears by instalments. He can only avoid the distress by immediately paying the full amount of the arrears, together with costs.

Distress is also available, but only after a court order, as a remedy for non-payment of rates and taxes. Indeed distress is the only remedy for non-payment of rates, and goes back to their first imposition under the reign of Queen Elizabeth I. Cases are still heard by the magistrates, as they were under the Elizabethan Act. What made sense originally, however, when the rate itself was made by the magistrates, does not do so today.

Akin to distress is the enforcement of a court order to pay money by the levying of execution upon the goods of the debtor. This occurs only after a court has pronounced judgment in favour of the creditor and the debtor has failed to pay up or, where an instalment order was made, has failed to meet the instalments. The goods can be seized by the bailiff, but normally he takes 'walking possession'. Having inspected the debtor's goods and taken an inventory, the bailiff leaves the premises – first telling the debtor that he must not part with any of the goods. The bailiff visits the premises from time to time to make sure the goods have not been interfered with. If this is not sufficient to compel payment, the goods can be sold by the bailiff, but this only occurs in a tiny proportion of cases. Where it does occur the disruption of the debtor's household by removal of his furniture may far outweigh any advantage accruing to the creditor by the removal and sale. The Under-sheriffs' Association has urged a change in the law to enable bailiffs to leave on debtors' premises sufficient furniture and other goods to prevent disruption of the household. They point out that many household effects have far less intrinsic value when removed for sale than their worth in the home, and that there would be little justification or need for their removal but for a creditor's insistence.

There are many different ways of levying distress or execution. The various remedies have developed over the centuries and have never been integrated or co-ordinated, though the officials themselves do, where possible, make attempts to avoid duplication.

Nevertheless it remains true that in this sphere, as in other aspects of enforcement of debts, the existence of a multiple debtor often leads to what the Payne Committee called a free-for-all or catch-as-catch-can.

EQUATING DEBT TO CRIME

Many people are surprised to find that civil debts are often recoverable in Magistrates' Courts (popularly known as Police Courts). While magistrates were the effective local government authority from the end of the Middle Ages to the nineteenth century, they are now primarily thought of as part of the machinery of criminal law. Yet proceedings for recovery of money due for reasons quite unconnected with crime still fall to be brought before them. Debts due under Acts of Parliament, or under contract to Government departments, local authorities or other public bodies, are recoverable in this way. So are income tax and other taxes, and even some debts due to private individuals. A debt for a refrigerator can be enforced only in a civil court if it was bought from a private trader but in a Magistrates' Court if from an electricity or gas board. Again, if a car knocks down a fence on private property, the driver may be sued in the County Court; but if an identical fence encloses property of a local authority, the claim for compensation will be brought in the Magistrates' Court. Apart from being capricious, and only explicable on historical grounds, these differences lead to confusion in the minds of the public. There is inevitably a stigma attached to being brought before the 'beaks' on a summons served by a police officer. This is exacerbated, if, as may happen, the hearing is sandwiched between purely criminal matters. While the magistrates may set aside a separate day for the hearing, for example of rates summonses (sometimes numbering several hundreds), this will not apply to the isolated proceeding for civil debt. It is sometimes argued, in defence of the present system, that proceedings in a Magistrates' Court are cheaper, quicker and less formal. There may be some truth in this, though the cheapness is more apparent than real since the community subsidises the creditor before a Magistrates' Court by providing the services of magistrates, police officers and other officials at a nominal charge. In some areas County Courts are considered quicker.

Another way in which civil debt enforcement is equated to crime is in the use of imprisonment. In 1962 nearly 8,000 debtors were imprisoned under orders of County Courts. This was more than one-seventh of the total number of persons sent to prison, borstal or detention centres upon sentences for crime from all criminal courts. By 1967, however, the number imprisoned dropped to less than half the 1962 figure. The present law of imprisonment for debt dates from the Debtors Act of 1869. Before then debtors could be imprisoned without court order following arrest by a sheriff's officer. Debtors' prisons such as the Marshalsea and the Fleet existed all over the country. When Parliament was debating the Act of 1869, many M.P.s felt that imprisonment should be abolished completely, but in the end it was decided to retain it for cases of contumacy. In general therefore a committal order to prison can only be made where the debtor has the means, or has had the means, to pay the debt and has flouted the order of the court. In some cases contumacy need not be proved, as for example where on distress for rates it is found that there are insufficient goods to satisfy the debt.

The treatment of recalcitrant debtors by imprisoning them as if they were criminals has been much criticised. A high proportion of those imprisoned are inadequate personalities whose failure is congenital rather than wilful. Imprisonment causes hardship to both the debtor and his family, and clearly makes it difficult if not impossible for him to meet current and future debts. It is uneconomic from the community's point of view. Prisoners are not engaged in productive work, and cost something like £15 a week to keep, disregarding capital costs of the prison establishment.

Debtors who find themselves in prison are usually there either because they have developed a fixed resolve, often based on emotional grounds, not to pay the debt although they have the means, or because they are of low mental calibre or inadequate personality. The person who perhaps ought to be there stays outside because he knows just how far he can go without unpleasantness to himself. He was described in this way in the Payne Report:

> A debtor who is experienced in the debtors' court knows that the County Court Judge is most reluctant to make any order which will result in a debtor going to prison and consequently, when a committal order is made, it is usually suspended on condition of payment of a much smaller monthly instalment than would be ordered if no committal order were attached. Such a debtor will ignore the summons, the judgment, the judgment summons and the notice of commitment, and will not normally make any payment until at the eleventh hour the bailiff arrives to arrest him. He will then pay what is outstanding on the warrant and the process may start all over again.

The Report adds that in such cases the committal order is not so much a weapon in the hands of the court or the creditor as in the hands of the debtor, who can by these tactics obtain several years credit for a debt which he may have contracted to pay immediately or by instalments over a much shorter period.

There is evidence to suggest that not merely may debt be equated with crime, but in some cases it may be punished more severely. Every year people are imprisoned for failure to pay debts of only a few shillings whereas for the theft of much greater amounts a first offender would be most unlikely to be sent to prison.

THE PAYNE REPORT

In 1965 Lord Chancellor Gardiner appointed a Committee under Mr Justice Payne to examine the law relating to debt enforcement, and the results of the Committee's exhaustive survey were published some four years later. The Committee were asked to turn their attention first to the question of imprisonment, and gave a preliminary finding on this in 1966. It was their unanimous conclusion that committal to prison under the Debtors Act 1869 and the judgment summons procedure in the County Court should be abolished. This was forthwith announced to the House of Commons, although at the time of writing it has not yet been translated into law. The Committee was not unanimous when it came to the question of imprisonment for failure to make payments under a Magistrates' Court order for the maintenance of a wife or children. Apart from the question of maintenance orders, however, all members of the Committee considered imprisonment for civil debt to be an outdated, often unjust and inappropriate method of enforcement. They were unable to accept that the vast structure of credit trading could depend on the threat of imprisonment even if all prisoners were shown to be deliberate defaulters. To the argument that the ultimate deterrent of imprisonment was the most effective means of ensuring payment the Committee rejoined that its other recommendations should provide an equally effective system.

Naturally the main concern of the Payne Committee was to put forward proposals for a rational and co-ordinated debt enforcement system (outside the law of bankruptcy, with which they were not concerned).

The key to the Payne Committee's proposals is the County Court. There has always been a monetary limit on the claims which could be pursued in a County Court. Within this limit, at present £500, the Committee recommends that the County Court should have exclusive jurisdiction so far as practicable. Up to this limit therefore the jurisdiction of the High Court to hear actions for the recovery of debt would be taken away. So would that of the Magistrates' Courts except in matrimonial and affiliation cases or where an order for the payment of money was incidental to criminal proceedings. This incidentally would involve giving tax officers a right of audience in the County Court corresponding to that now enjoyed by them in Magistrates' Courts on tax recovery summonses.

Having secured that so far as practicable judgments for debt would be given in the County Court and nowhere else, the Committee come to their main recommendation. The job of enforcing judgments would be given to a new organisation attached to the County Courts and coming under the jurisdiction of the Lord Chancellor. The Committee show hesitation about whether this would be an administrative office or a type of court. They appear to decide that it would have most of the characteristics of a court but nevertheless elect to call it the Enforcement Office. All money judgments from all courts would be channelled and enforced through the Enforcement Office. To enable it to operate effectively, and to make up for the abolition of imprisonment for debt, a range of new or strengthened procedures are recommended. These include a general system of attachment of earnings, a procedure akin to that in bankruptcy for extracting information as to the debtor's means, and an extension of the social services to give help to inadequate debtors coupled with strengthened provisions for administration of a debtor's assets short of bankruptcy.

THE ENFORCEMENT OFFICE

Under the proposals of the Payne Committee the Enforcement Office would be a Court of Record whose orders would have the same force as those of any other court. Proceedings for the enforcement of judgment debts, wherever the debt was contracted or the judgment given, would be taken in the Enforcement Office in the district in which the debtor resided or carried on business. This will ensure that the appropriate local office will have all enforcement matters against that debtor under its control. It will be aware of his total indebtedness and be able to supervise the orderly liquidation of debt and determine priorities and disputes between creditors. It will also be able to protect the debtor against undue hardship or harassment. Each local office will be in charge of an Enforcement Officer. The Registrar of the County Court to which the office is attached will perform this function, and the Enforcement Office will be staffed by the County Court clerks and bailiffs. The Enforcement Officer will make an order for enforcement as soon as an application for this, duly completed and signed, is received.

One of the essential features of the scheme is that the Enforcement Office should be able to find out what property and income the debtor has at his disposal and what are his financial commitments and general circumstances. Under the present system this information is not usually known either to creditors or the court. Under the new scheme the debtor will be required to make a full disclosure of his affairs by completing a questionnaire and when required attending for questioning. The debtor's answers will be made known to the creditors, but he could avoid having to give them by paying the debt. The questionnaire should state this clearly and be used as an additional method of securing payment. The questions envisaged are far-reaching. It will be for many debtors a major operation to complete a form which requires such information as a statement of his goods 'including the main items of furniture and other household effects', and a description of 'his assets, capital or property'. Only eight days is to be allowed for completion. Failure to complete the questionnaire, or any other disobedience of the Enforcement Office's orders, would be treated as contempt of court and punishable accordingly.

It is proposed that the Enforcement Office should have a large armoury of weapons at its disposal to ensure that the debtor pays up to the best of his ability. These weapons include control and attachment of assets, attachment of earnings, execution upon goods, attachment of debts owed to the debtor, determination of hire-purchase and other agreements and the appointment of a receiver. No method would be used except on the application of the creditor, who could at any time require enforcement proceedings in the case of his own debt to be discontinued. If there is any change in the debtor's position, as by the receipt of a legacy or other windfall, the creditor can apply to the Enforcement Office for a variation in any instalment or other order. It is an essential part of the scheme that the Enforcement Office should be able to make one instalment order for the discharge of a number of debts and to distribute the proceeds among the creditors *pro rata*. The Enforcement Office would be financed by fees, but a creditor would only be required to pay one fee (at the time of his application), and should not be required to pay more however many steps may be required for the enforcement of his debt. The amount of this fee would be added to the judgment debt. Apart from thus having his debt increased, the debtor should not be required to pay any fees. An appeal would lie from any decision of the Enforcement Office to the County Court Judge.

These recommendations clearly represent a thoughtful and

carefully worked out solution to the problems surrounding debt recovery. Certain anxieties remain however. Perhaps the most disquieting feature of the Committee's proposals is that they may tend to make the position of the ordinary judgment debtor resemble that of the bankrupt in the degree to which his affairs are subject to official interference and publicity. Apart from this one may detect some signs of reformer's grandeur in the desire to set up a new department or court. Since the staff, premises and general superintendence will be those of the County Court it is difficult to see why the new system could not simply be regarded as an additional function of the County Court. The only feature missing is a central office from which the necessary work of co-ordination could be done. There is no reason why a County Court Enforcement Office should not be set up to carry out this co-ordinating function; alternatively it could be made a function of the Lord Chancellor's Department itself.

Another point of controversy, revealed as such in the report itself, is whether the Enforcement Office should be given full discretion to pursue such remedies as it thinks fit or whether, as the majority of the Committee thought, the initiative should lie with the creditor. The Committee felt that a private debt does not cease to be private by being transformed into a judgment debt, and a judgment does not impose the duty of collecting the debt upon the state. Against this view, a member of the Committee, Mr Registrar Bryson, made powerful objection from his own experience. A big court would receive over a thousand applications a week for enforcement. If every step had to be authorised by the creditors the system would not work in the face of almost insuperable administrative difficulties. He also felt that with the abolition of imprisonment as a sanction creditors would expect a much better service, and that this could only be achieved by giving the Enforcement Office a free rein. While there is much weight in this view, it seems clear that if it had this role the Enforcement Office would in effect be an instrument of the creditor and could scarcely be presided over by a judicial officer such as the Registrar of the County Court.

RAIDING THE PAY-PACKET

Attachment of earnings is a thorny subject. It seems simple and easy to ensure that a man pays his debts by directing his employer to make deductions from his pay and hand them over to the creditor. Against this is a long-standing principle that the wage-packet is inviolable. The Truck Acts date back to the fifteenth century, and require wages to be paid in cash and not in kind. An Act of 1870 prohibited deductions from wages being made by court order. Nevertheless the twentieth century has seen breaches of the inviolability of the pay-packet. As the law stands now a number of deductions are permitted, from PAYE and National Insurance to payments under affiliation and other maintenance orders and fines and legal aid contributions. This list is virtually exhaustive, however, and attachment of earnings is not generally available as a means of debt collection.

There is mounting pressure to change the law so that this easy remedy can be available to all creditors. A number of lawyers' organisations are in favour of the change, which is even supported by the National Council for Civil Liberties. Perhaps surprisingly, the TUC is also a supporter, having recently reversed its long-standing opposition. This opposition was based on the fear that workers whose wages were attached to enforce payment of debts would be prejudiced in the eyes of their employers and might be liable to dismissal. The chances of securing new employment in such circumstances would also be reduced. The TUC now feel that the stigma attaching to debt has gone and this, together with the long-continuing period of full employment, has removed their objections.

The Payne Committee recommended that the Enforcement Office should have power to make an attachment of earnings order against any judgment debtor in receipt of wages or salary. For special reasons, there would be an exception for merchant seamen. It is doubtful whether this recommendation will be adopted, since there are still formidable obstacles. First, there are the practical difficulties. These mainly concern the ease with which a worker can evade an attachment of earnings order simply by changing his employment. No real solution to this problem has been found. Apart from practical difficulties, there are strong objections to the system on the grounds that it is an indefensible breach of privacy and causes unwarrantable inconvenience to employers.

Despite the views of the TUC it may be doubted whether employers are really indifferent to their employees being debt-defaulters. The fact that a man has failed to manage his affairs properly and has become the subject of enforcement proceedings does not redound to his credit and suggests improvidence or worse. This may not matter with a manual worker, but for clerical and administrative grades it is serious. The Payne Committee considered whether it would be possible to provide protection for employees against dismissal simply because they had become subject to enforcement proceedings. No practicable way of achieving this was found. While there may be a case justifying the present system under which orders for the maintenance of mothers and children can be enforced by attachment of earnings, these reasons do not apply to the ordinary commercial creditor. If he has given credit, he has done so on a commercial basis and with his eyes open. There seems no reason to penalise the debtor by making his financial embarrassment known to his employers.

Nor is there any reason why employers should be forced to become debt collectors on behalf of commercial creditors. The Payne Committee offer a derisory sixpence to the employer for each payment remitted to the creditor under an attachment order. They admit that this would in no way cover the actual cost.

PROTECTING THE PRODIGAL

The conclusion is surely obvious that except where humanitarian reasons compel the use of every weapon to ensure payment of a debt the privacy of the debtor should be protected as far as possible. Commercial traders should not be able to rely on a man's employers to get them out of trouble, or be able to ruin an employee's prospects in his job.

On the other hand there may be a case for protecting the debtor from himself by restricting, in bad cases, the ability to contract new debts. Other instruments are the administration order and an extension of welfare advisory services.

Administration proceedings can be brought in the County Court at present, and the Payne Committee recommend an extended use of them. This will enable all the debts of the debtor, whether the subject of judgments or not, to be listed and an orderly scheme for the distribution of assets drawn up. The procedure is akin to bankruptcy, but without its drastic consequences. Nevertheless the Enforcement Officer would have a discretion in enforcement proceedings to prohibit the debtor from entering into hire-purchase arrangements and restricting his credit. The Committee rejected a proposal to enable credit restrictions to be made apart from administration proceedings. They felt that where the debtor's state of insolvency did not warrant the making of an administration order it was sufficient to rely on the growing practice of making judgment debts known through credit information bureaux, trade magazines and the like to give sufficient notice to prospective creditors. We have not yet reached the position of the ancient Romans, under which a prodigal who wasted his substance could be placed under interdict.

A MONSTER COMPUTER?

Some people have looked to the computer to solve the problem of debt enforcement. At present even the debts owed by a person to the state are dealt with in separate compartments. Income tax is accounted for and paid over by a separate machinery from that applied to National Insurance contributions. Why should there not be a single computer file for all state transactions by any one citizen? His whole indebtedness could then be dealt with as one transaction, and debt collection simplified. There are many different financial transactions a man may have with the state nowadays, and, through the Post Office Savings Bank or National Giro, he may use the state as banker. There are superficial attractions about combining all these debits and credits into one account. Perhaps some day this may come, but those who oppose it fear the dangers to the individual that could flow from all his affairs being recorded in a single file, putting him at the mercy of any official having access to it who chooses to abuse his knowledge.

If such a centralised system of accounting were, however, created, and in connection with it the state kept track of the whereabouts of every citizen, many of the problems of attachment of earnings would disappear. Change of job would not avail the debtor. His employer need not become aware of his indebtedness, since there would be a coding system under which one deduction would be made by the employer to cover any number of debts owed either to the state or to private creditors. The employer would remit the deducted amount to the central computer office, which would then distribute the constituent parts to those entitled to receive them. This would be a commonsense system, but the overtones of tyranny and loss of privacy will probably prevent its adoption – at least for the time being.

8

Children in Trouble

Legal rules, enforced by legal process, are the means by which society protects itself against the antisocial. The formal apparatus of law, lawyers and courts deals adequately with wrongdoers of full age and capacity. For others, particularly children, we are nowadays inclined to use other means. A little over a hundred years ago a child could be hanged in England for stealing a loaf of bread. Early in this century prison for very young offenders was still the rule; and only in 1932 was the minimum age of criminal responsibility raised to eight years, and a few years later to ten.

The first major step towards treating accused children differently from adults was taken sixty years ago with the establishment of the juvenile courts. Here proceedings are simplified so that young people and their parents can understand what is happening. The court normally consists of three lay magistrates specially selected for their experience and sympathy with the problems of the young. There are many kinds of orders which the court can make, including fine, detention in a detention centre, probation, attendance at an attendance centre, and sending away to an approved school. Though informal, the proceedings of the juvenile court are judicial in nature, and where the accused pleads not guilty he has to be acquitted if the prosecution cannot prove beyond reasonable doubt that he has committed the offence charged. There is a 'tariff' of court orders, which though quite unofficial is well understood by those concerned. On the first appearance a conditional discharge is the most frequent decision (in two-thirds of cases). For second and third appearances probation orders are most common (in about half the cases). Young people appearing for a fourth or subsequent time are most often sent to an approved school or ordered to be placed in charge of a 'fit person'–usually the local authority.

Not surprisingly, this tariff is usually viewed by children and their parents as representing a scale of punishments rather than corrective or remedial methods.

This brings us to the nub of current arguments on juvenile delinquency. Should punishment or cure be the main object of the system? The answer largely depends on what are looked upon as the true causes of delinquency. The present official view is indicated by the following passage from a white paper, *Children in Trouble* published by the Home Office in 1968:

> Juvenile delinquency has no single cause, manifestation or cure. Its origins are many, and the range of behaviour which it covers is equally wide. At some points it merges almost imperceptibly with behaviour which does not contravene the law. A child's behaviour is influenced by genetic, emotional and intellectual factors, his maturity, and his family, school, neighbourhood and wider social setting. It is probably a minority of children who grow up without ever misbehaving in ways which may be contrary to the law. Frequently such behaviour is no more than an incident in the pattern of a child's normal development. But sometimes it is a response to unsatisfactory family or social circumstances, a result of boredom in or out of school, an indication of maladjustment or immaturity, or a symptom of a deviant, damaged or abnormal personality.

It is recognised that some types of delinquency are 'normal' in the sense that they do not spring from defects in personality or environment. Workers such as Glueck have demonstrated what is perhaps obvious, that delinquency in childhood and adolescence is at least partly a form of seeking for danger, adventure, independence and self-assertion in a culture which provides inadequate outlets for these natural qualities. Discipline and punishment is clearly not inappropriate in such cases.

Most delinquency can, however, be traced to causes for which the child is in no way to blame, and control of the consequences of which may well be beyond him. Here punishment is not merely wrong; it is useless. Very many cases of delinquency among boys show a defective family background. The boy brought up in a home where the father is missing, or hopelessly inadequate; where love and security are absent, and emotional problems are exacerbated by poverty, can scarcely be blamed for his antisocial acts. Let anyone who is disposed to blame him ponder the facts of just one case, taken from a recent study by Pauline Shapiro, in which only the name of the family concerned is fictitious.

> The Clancys are well known to most social agencies in the city as a typical problem family. They live in a three room back-to-back in a twilight area. It has running cold water and, in the yard, a wash-house and three lavatories for eight families. Mr Clancy is thirty years old, in poor health, blind in one eye and with recurrent ulcers in the groin. Social agencies dub him work-shy. He is seldom home, takes his meals and his drinks out and is said to go round with other women, on one occasion leaving his family for some weeks. His wife is twenty-nine, pregnant with her ninth child, and looks extremely shabby and much older than her years. She seems to be of poor intelligence, and is quite unable to manage money, of which she has too little, or children, of whom she has too many. Her method of discipline for the children is at one time to ignore difficulties and disobedience, at another to shout and clout.

If one of Mrs Clancy's children gets into a scrape with the law, society has an obvious problem over what to do with him. It is true that he probably would not have got into the scrape if, in the classic phrase, there had been a policeman standing at his elbow. This does not mean that the full rigours of trial and punishment are the appropriate response. It does not even mean that he should necessarily be brought before the special tribunal for young offenders, the juvenile court. In most cases of crime the decision on whether to prosecute rests with the police, and in many areas the police have for some years exercised considerable discretion over bringing juveniles before the court–at least where they have no criminal record. A procedure has grown up whereby the police will in suitable cases administer a caution to a young offender instead of bringing him before the courts. In London this system of cautions has reached a considerable degree of elaboration. For its operation a small bureau of specially selected and trained police officers under the control of a Chief Inspector has been set up in each division of the Metropolitan Police District. When a young offender is arrested he is taken to the police station and the offence is investigated in the normal manner. In a suitable case he will then be released into the custody of his parents while the police obtain information about him. If in the light of this it seems appropriate that, instead of bringing him before the court, he should be given a ticking-off by a policeman and warned about the consequences of future misbehaviour this is done. It is only done, however, if the offence is admitted, the parents agree, and any aggrieved third party also agrees. The caution is given formally at the police station by a Chief Inspector in uniform, thus impressing upon the young person the seriousness of the matter. This practice of cautioning has official approval of course, but is followed very unevenly throughout the country. In Devon and Cornwall, for example, two child offenders out of three are cautioned. At the other end of the scale, there is more than one area in Britain where only one in twenty is cautioned and the other nineteen are taken to court.

Methods of dealing with juvenile crime which have grown up since the last war have not succeeded in preventing a very steep rise in the number of offences. The total of young persons found guilty of indictable offences (that is those of a more serious nature) has risen from about 28,000 in 1938 to nearly 63,000 by 1965. There has been a similar increase in adult crime. The feeling that the system of dealing with juvenile delinquency placed too much emphasis on criminal rather than remedial aspects, and was perhaps unsuccessful for that reason, led to far-reaching reforms in 1969. It is beyond the purpose of this book to deal comprehensively with these reforms. We can look only at features close to our main theme–the area within which the individual tangles with legal process. Whatever is done to the young delinquent by the state must of course be done under legal powers, but it need not be done by legal process as we traditionally know it. Recent reforms are of special interest in their relationship to concepts long regarded as fundamental to British justice, such as no detention without trial, the presumption of innocence, the awarding of punishment by a judicial agency, the safeguarding of individual liberty by the courts, the concept of law as the embodiment of common morality, and the doctrine of the individual's responsibility for his acts. The 1969 reforms in the treatment of young delinquents depart radically from many of these principles. Whether they are right to do so is an issue of vital concern.

GUILT AND THE CHILD

The underlying purpose of the 1969 reforms is to make the treatment of young delinquents a civil rather than a criminal matter or, as it is inaccurately put, to 'get them out of the courts'. The word 'crime' sounds harshly in our sensitive modern ears, but it is worth considering for a moment its dictionary meaning. This is 'the violation of a right when considered in reference to the evil tendency of such violation as regards the community at large; an act or default which tends to the prejudice of the community and is forbidden by law on pain of punishment inflicted at the instance of the state'. A crime, in other words, is an antisocial act.

The law has always recognised that an infant of tender years is incapable of forming the evil intent necessary for the commission of a crime. Our forefathers regarded the attainment of a child's seventh birthday as the moment when it should cease to be treated as incapable of crime. Between then and the fourteenth birthday there was a presumption of incapacity which could be rebutted by evidence of the child's ability to distinguish good and evil. It is a curious paradox that the introduction of compulsory schooling for all should have led to successive increases, during this century, in the age below which a child is presumed incapable of crime. This age has been successively raised to eight, then ten, and now in the 1969 reforms to fourteen. The answer to the paradox is that we are witnessing a shift in the rationale of this age limit. It has ceased to represent a rule of thumb for judging a child's presumed ability to distinguish good and evil. Instead it has become a means of shielding young people from the rigours of criminal process and punishment. This is shown by the language used in the 1969 provisions, which state that no person shall be *charged* with an offence by reason of anything done or omitted while he was under the age of fourteen. The prohibition does not apply to homicide, and the age limit of fourteen is to be reached in stages. This is necessary because the reforms are expected to require many more local authority officials to carry them out, and for some time to come the effective age limit will in fact be twelve and not fourteen.

The reforms also place restrictions on the prosecution of adolescents under the age of seventeen. The consent of a magistrate will be necessary, and this can only be applied for by a police officer or public official. The normal right of an aggrieved private citizen to prosecute where the authorities decline to do so is thus taken away. The local authority must always be consulted before a prosecution is authorised and the magistrate can only give authority if there are special reasons relating to the offence or the offender. The offence must be of a serious type, such as homicide, or a type causing much public concern. Otherwise consent to prosecution can only be given where the circumstances of the offender justify this, e.g. where his record indicates that action without the backing of a court order would not be likely to succeed.

Those who support the reformers' desire to 'get young people out of the courts' feel that the atmosphere of a court, even a juvenile court, is not a thing to which children should be subjected. As Lady Birk put it in the House of Lords debates on the 1969 reforms:

> The trouble has arisen here because as a society and as a country we are still glued to the principle of court referral. If we stick rigidly to legal niceties in this human field, which above all others requires the greatest flexibility and informality, it means that justice in the deeper sense is not necessarily done, although superficially it may appear to be done.

It is true that despite the many efforts made to humanise them, juvenile courts retain a good deal of formality, and tend to be crowded with onlookers such as probation officers, children's officers, police, reporters and visitors. The accused young people are made to stand in front of the magistrates, who sit on a raised dais and seldom feel able to come round and talk to the child or his parents (who sit behind him) in an informal way.

If the real objection to treating young delinquents as criminals is the nature of court proceedings it might be thought that the obvious reform would be to simplify the method of trial rather than doing away with the concept of guilt altogether. One commentator criticised the way right and wrong, guilt and innocence, are 'vanishing into a bureaucratic cloud'. There is much force in this comment; indeed the 1969 proposals are a remarkable example of the British habit of getting round procedural defects (which are troublesome to change) by attacking principle.

'CARE, PROTECTION OR CONTROL'

The muddled thinking behind the 1969 reforms goes much further. They have not in fact succeeded in getting the children out of the courts, because we find that while a child may not be prosecuted for an offence the question whether he committed the offence remains relevant. This is because the treatment of the offender, at least where it involves any compulsion, cannot be undertaken without a court order. One of the new grounds on which the court can make an order is that the child is guilty of an offence. If he denies having committed the offence it will be necessary to prove it in the same way as formerly, and if after hearing evidence the court is not satisfied that will be the end of the proceedings. The result of these elaborate reforms is therefore to leave the law substantially unchanged on this point, but to leave everyone concerned in considerable perplexity as to whether guilt has been established or not–or indeed as to what meaning is left in the word 'guilt'. The proceedings are described as 'civil' not criminal in nature, but if a child is found in civil proceedings to have committed an offence is he guilty or not? A nice philosophical conundrum!

The main purpose of the new provisions is that a court order should only be made against a child if he is in need of care, protection or control. If in putting forward these reforms the Government had had the courage of their convictions and taken away altogether the need to determine whether an offence had been committed they would at least have had a logical case. As it was they landed themselves in an absurdity the full extent of which is not, at the time of writing, known. When the Bill containing the 1969 reforms reached the House of Lords it provided that an order against a child accused of an offence could only be made if it was established both that the offence had been committed and that the child was in need of care or control. This was attacked in the House as being bound to lead to 'obvious injustice' where two children had been involved in an offence. If one came from a good home, and was not in need of care or control, he would not be brought before the court. His companion on the other hand might well come from a very bad home and be brought to court because he clearly needed help. As Lord Jellicoe put it, 'I cannot but feel that this will strike the children concerned, and also their parents, as an obvious and glaring injustice'. By a narrow majority their lordships agreed with him and altered the Bill to enable orders to be made against both children in such cases. On Government insistence this decision was subsequently reversed.

These difficulties illustrate the confusion prevailing as to the true role of the courts in dealing with young delinquents at the present day. The 1969 reforms, as we shall see, reject the traditional idea that it is for the court to determine the type of treatment to be meted out to the young offender, and place decisions on this in the hands of the local authority. Since such treatment involves the element of compulsion, however, the reformers wish to keep the court as a body for determining whether it is right to subject the child to compulsory treatment. In other words the juvenile court magistrate is seen as a protector of the child's liberty, which cannot be taken away or placed at risk unless the magistrate thinks this is justified. The traditional working-class view of the courts is of course the reverse of this; they are seen as dealing out punishment themselves and not as restraining its being dealt out by other people. It is a measure of the clumsiness of the 1969 reforms that their authors did not foresee the implausibility of presenting the courts in this reverse role.

THE END OF THE APPROVED SCHOOL

Approved schools have been with us for nearly forty years, as successors to reformatories and industrial schools. They are scheduled to disappear under the 1969 reforms. They have come to be associated in the public mind with strong discipline of a rather old-fashioned nature and so they are to go. To prepare the public for this the Home Office has been eager in recent years to give publicity to over-harsh conditions in some schools. The prime example of this was the Court Lees approved school in Surrey, where several members of the staff were suspended following findings of excessive caning.

The abolition of approved schools is part of a scheme for removing all the legal distinctions between boarding establishments for delinquent or deprived children and young persons. In future, wherever it is thought necessary by the juvenile court to remove a young offender from his home environment this will be done by means of an order placing him in the care of the local authority in whose area he lives. It will be for the local authority to decide what is to be done with him, and it will have an extremely flexible range of facilities to choose from.

Under the system prevailing before the 1969 reforms over twenty thousand children under eighteen were at any one time in the care of local authorities under 'fit person' orders. The new proposals are an extension of this system, by which all young people whose home conditions are inadequate will be placed in the same legal category, whether they are offenders, absconders or innocent victims of ill-treatment or moral danger.

Under the new reforms local authorities will be required to develop a system of residential homes to be known as community homes. These may be run by the local authority themselves or by voluntary agencies. Community homes will be varied in nature, and will in fact be, under another guise, the previously existing local authority children's homes and hostels, remand homes, reception and remand centres, local authority and voluntary approved schools, and some voluntary children's homes which regularly accommodate children in care. It is an important feature of the system that by no means all the young people placed by the juvenile court in the care of the local authority will be accommodated in these community homes. Half, at least, are expected to be boarded out with foster parents or otherwise cared for privately. In special cases it will even be possible for them to go on living with their parents, on trial as it were. Committal to the local authority may remain effective up to the nineteenth birthday.

Once the juvenile court has made a care order it will be for the local authority to decide from time to time during the duration of the order how the youngster is to be treated. He may, at the discretion of the local authority, be moved around from foster parents to a residential home and then, if his behaviour seems to warrant it, to an establishment differing hardly at all from the present approved school. His liberty may be confined, and he may be placed in what are euphemistically described as 'secure conditions' whenever the local authority thinks fit. There are obvious merits in this increased degree of flexibility. Local authority children's officers will get to know the child and can respond sensitively and quickly to his changing needs. With the disappearance of the approved school order there will also disappear the stigma attaching to it. The wide variety of circumstances in which a care order can be made should take away the idea of punishment altogether.

LIBERTY–WHO SHOULD DECIDE?

The 1969 reforms undoubtedly mark a radical departure from traditional principles of British justice. This is done of course with the best motives and may be justified. Nothing can disguise, however, the fact that it takes away from the court the jurisdiction of deciding whether at any given moment a young person up to the age of nineteen should be incarcerated or set at liberty.

Admittedly there are safeguards. The young person concerned, or his parent, may at any time apply to the juvenile court for the revocation of a care order. So of course may the local authority, and every six months they are required to review the case to see whether the order should be revoked. Furthermore it is possible, though by no means certain, that provision will be made requiring local authorities to review at intervals any permission they have given for a child to be placed in secure accommodation, and to conduct that review through a committee which includes an independent person.

How effective these safeguards will prove in practice one cannot tell. Where it has been found necessary to take a youngster away from his parents it is hardly likely that they will feel sufficient concern for his liberty to initiate an application to the court. The youngster himself may sometimes be of the type who is prepared to cause trouble by making applications to the court as often as he can, that is every three months. In most cases however, youth, sub-normality or ignorance will probably insure that the powers of the local authority officials are not effectively checked. All this is in marked contrast to the previous system, under which it was clear to the juvenile courts and everyone else whether or not the child's liberty was being taken away, and an appeal lay to a higher judicial tribunal.

Many will sympathise with the comments of Lord Hamilton of Dalzell in the House of Lords proceedings on the 1969 reforms. Speaking with experience as a juvenile court magistrate, he complained that under the new arrangements everything was being subordinated to 'the all-embracing, all-powerful local authority machine'. It is hardly an answer to say, as Lady Wootton did in the same debate, that the position is no worse than for an ordinary child who could be sent to a boarding school by his parents any day. 'He does not have the freedom to choose his own residence but no one suggests that he is deprived of his liberty.' It is surely wrong to equate a large bureaucratic organisation, however well-meaning, with flesh and blood parents.

A NEW HALF-WAY HOUSE

Another novel feature of the 1969 reform is less open to criticism. It is the attempt to provide a half-way house between leaving the child in its home environment and removing him from home altogether. Where the circumstances do not justify a care order, the juvenile court can make an order placing the child under supervision. Normally the supervisor will be a local authority children's officer, who is required by law to 'advise, assist and befriend' the youngster. (One complaint made in Parliament was that the word 'love' was not added.)

Where a supervision order is made new methods of intermediate treatment will be possible. The first type of treatment will involve attendance for a period fixed by the court, not exceeding one month in any one year. The youngster will be required to attend for a number of evenings, or perhaps entire weekends, for training or participation in a work project or community service. The idea is to bring him into contact with people from whom he may learn a good example, and to get him interested in constructive activities.

The more strict type of intermediate treatment will involve residence away from home for a period of not more than three months. This will enable the child to be given treatment, or removed from home during a critical period. So far these are only paper schemes, not worked out in any detail. They hold obvious promise, however, and mark the progress of an idea which may well be the key to the treatment of delinquency–at least where serious mental or personality defects are absent. This is that instead of placing delinquents together in a home or boarding establishment, where they can each make one another's characters worse, they should be placed with people who can set them an example. Lady Wootton remarked that her long experience in juvenile courts had convinced her that we make more delinquents in the waiting room than we ever cure in the courtroom.

SUMMING UP

We cannot yet judge whether on balance the 1969 reforms will prove beneficial. So much depends on how they are operated. They may enmesh young people in a bureaucratic fog, which will do little to straighten out their difficulties. They may, on the other hand, by removing the aura of criminality from youthful misdeeds, help to save their perpetrators from becoming real criminals later on. Let us hope that on balance they will offer a better deal for Mrs Clancy's children.

9

The Innocent Accused

Especially to be pitied are those who get entangled in the criminal law through no fault of their own. It will not necessarily avail them that they are guiltless of any offence, and although they may in the end succeed in establishing their innocence they will suffer in mind and pocket on the way. When it was suggested to Dr Johnson that truth would always bear examination he retorted that this might be so, but it was painful to be forced to defend it. 'Consider, Sir, how should you like, though conscious of your innocence, to be tried before a jury for a capital crime, once a week.' In some cases, as history records, innocence fails to prove itself and to the distress of a trial is added the agony of false conviction and unmerited punishment. Naturally enough, legal reformers give close attention to these matters and proposals to improve the safeguards for the innocent are constantly being made.

Ignorance, as Browning said, is not innocence. We are not concerned in this chapter with the person who transgresses unwittingly because he was unaware of a legal prohibition, and had no reason to suspect its existence. In so far as he may have any grievance against authority for not ensuring that the prohibition was drawn to his notice, its remedy lies along lines discussed in Chapter 2. Let us now look at the individual who is completely free from guilt, or even involvement in crime, and see how, if he is unlucky, the processes of law may bring him down.

INTERROGATION OF SUSPECTS

When the finger of suspicion points at a person the first consequence will be police questioning. It is here that errors may creep in which could ultimately lead to wrongful conviction. Most policemen pride themselves on a sixth sense where suspects are concerned, and very few are interested in bringing the wrong person before the court. What they sometimes do, through excess of zeal, is to bend the rules to gain evidence against a suspect who they are convinced is guilty. It is here that danger lies.

It is a principle of English justice that a suspected person is not obliged to answer questions which may incriminate him. The detection of crime would become impossible, however, if the police were effectively precluded from interrogation. The position therefore is that the police do ask questions, suspects usually answer them, and the result is admitted in evidence if the police have complied with rules first laid down by the judges in 1912.

The no-incrimination principle is an aspect of the fact that the system of English criminal procedure is accusatorial instead of being, as on the Continent, inquisitorial. In France, for example, serious crimes are subject to a searching preliminary inquiry by a judge who investigates every aspect and rigorously questions suspects. They are obliged to answer. At the trial itself the French judge again adopts an inquisitorial role, though the actual prosecution is conducted by an official appointed for the purpose. The view is being increasingly expressed that the British system is too kind to the guilty, and unnecessarily complicates investigation of crime. This is by no means a recent development. In the last century, Jeremy Bentham strongly criticised the principle of no self-incrimination. It was based, he said, on recollection of ancient barbarities accompanying the extraction of confessions. The reasons justifying it were 'the old woman's reason', that ''tis hard upon a man to be obliged to incriminate himself', and 'the fox hunter's reason', that it is unsporting. In the present day, 'Justice' (the British section of the International Commission of Jurists) has supported Bentham's view. After stating in 1960 that to deprive an accused person of his right to remain silent would be 'alien to the general conception of justice in this country', 'Justice' in a report published in 1967 recommended the abolition of the principle of no self-incrimination and the introduction of a new procedure of controlled compulsory interrogation before a magistrate.

The record of the interrogation would be admissible in evidence at any subsequent trial. Although the interrogation would be conducted in the presence of the magistrate he would not take on the role of interrogator, which would be performed by the police. The report suggests that if this procedure were adopted then as a general rule no statement made to the police by the accused, other than that recorded at the official interrogation, should be admissible in evidence at his trial.

Other influential voices have recently pleaded for abolition of the principle of no self-incrimination. Sir Norman Skelhorn, the Director of Public Prosecutions, suggested this at the Commonwealth Law Conference in 1965. In his view a person being questioned by the police, at least until he is charged with an offence, should be under an obligation to reply to their questions. The nature of this proposed obligation is obscure, since Sir Norman does not suggest that failure to answer police questions should be a criminal offence. Failure to answer would be a subject for comment at the trial of the accused, but the effect of this is difficult to predict. A citizen who knows his rights under the law, and is conscious of his innocence, is probably well advised to refuse to answer police questions–at least in the absence of his lawyer. His refusal can hardly be taken as evidence of guilt. Lord MacDermott, the Lord Chief Justice of Northern Ireland, has put forward proposals very similar to those of 'Justice'. In his view the police should have power to bring a suspect for questioning by them before a magistrate, who would see fair play, check the relevance of questions, and ensure that the interrogation was reasonably and properly conducted. He envisages that this would be a reserve power, which would not need to be used very often. Indeed it is unlikely that it would ever need to be used since its very existence would make it pointless for the suspect to resist questioning.

The proposals of 'Justice' and others represent a fundamental departure in traditions of fair play on which the British have long prided themselves. While it is true that under the present system the guilty may occasionally escape, freedom to refrain from answering police questions is a bulwark of liberty not lightly to be discarded. Certain it is that there can be no police state while this principle remains.

The Judges' Rules, referred to above, were revised in 1964 in a way which appears to allow greater freedom for police questioning. The Rules have not the force of law; they are administrative directions which the police are supposed to observe or risk disciplinary action. The only other sanction for breach of the Rules is that statements made by accused persons may be rendered inadmissible in evidence and therefore useless in securing a conviction. It has to be remembered, however, that apart from obtaining statements that can be used in evidence, the object of police questioning may well be to secure information which will lead to the discovery of facts which can be given in evidence independently of whether or not the Judges' Rules have been observed.

It is a long established rule of British law that no statement by an accused person is admissible in evidence against him unless it is shown by the prosecution to have been a *voluntary* statement, in the sense that it has not been obtained under oppression, threat, or inducement. The main purpose of the Judges' Rules is to ensure that these factors are not present, and for this the rules divide interrogations into three stages. The first stage lasts until the interrogator has accumulated evidence affording reasonable grounds for thinking that the suspect has committed an offence. During this stage no caution need be administered. Once, however, the police officer considers that he has sufficient evidence for suspicion he must administer a caution informing the suspect that he is not obliged to answer questions, but that if he does so his answers may be given in evidence. The third stage arises after a suspect has been charged with an offence. Further questioning is then permitted only in exceptional, though loosely defined, circumstances; and a further caution must be administered.

There has been much criticism of the revised Judges' Rules. The basic objection is that the need to administer cautions at specific stages renders an investigation artificial and hampers the police. They therefore tend to disregard the Rules, or look on them as a tiresome formality. One police officer is on record as saying that any of his colleagues who did not know the Judges' Rules would be a fool, but he would be even more of a fool if he adhered to them. Nevertheless the police, if asked in court whether they have complied with the rules, are unlikely to give a negative answer. Perjury is thus encouraged. One commentator, L. Hoffman, has argued against the whole idea of cautioning suspects:

> A caution would have a socially justifiable purpose only if it prevented innocent persons from making admissions which were false. It would be interesting to have some evidence of how likely this was to happen. What seems more probable is that the effect of the solemn and ancient formula is to make an innocent person say nothing for fear of incriminating himself, and thereby refrain from giving an explanation which would have satisfied the police.

Several commentators have recently urged the abolition of the Judges' Rules. These include Lord MacDermott, who feels that the courts should be left to determine, as a matter of law, whether evidence offered is admissible and, as a matter of discretion, whether it should be excluded in the interests of a fair trial. There seems, however, little point in abolishing the Rules, since the police would have to be given some guidance about the permissible mode of questioning. If the Judges' Rules were abolished it would be for the Home Office, as the executive branch having surveillance over the police, to issue instructions. It seems preferable in the interests of justice that if such instructions are to be given they should, as at present, be given by the judges rather than the executive. Certainly nothing must be done to encourage the police to think that they can use any means to extract evidence. There have been several recent inquiries which have established brutality by police seeking evidence. One of the most notorious was the case of the two Sheffield police officers in 1963 who were found by a tribunal to have been guilty of inflicting grievous bodily harm of a serious nature on two persons in custody. The tribunal found that 'the appellants' own evidence before us amounted in each case to a confession of deliberate, unprovoked, brutal and sustained assaults, with weapons of the nature of a truncheon and a short flexible piece of gut-like material, upon prisoners who were defenceless and did not retaliate, for the purpose of inducing confessions of crime.'

POWERS OF ARREST

If the innocent suspect gives unsatisfactory answers to police questioning, or asserts his right to remain silent, he may find himself arrested. It is important to the liberty of the individual that the cases where a power of arrest exists should be clearly known both to the citizen and the police. The citizen needs to know them not only to safeguard his own position, but also because (perhaps to his surprise) he has considerable powers of arrest himself.

Until modified by statute in 1967, the common law authorised any person to arrest anyone who committed a felony, or inflicted a dangerous wound, or perpetrated a breach of the peace, provided the act was done in his presence. The power also extended to attempted offences, and cases of suspicion where an offence had in fact been committed. The powers of the police were even wider than this at common law, but the whole position has been altered by the Criminal Justice Act of 1967. This abolishes distinctions between felony and misdemeanour, and creates a new concept, the 'arrestable offence'. Any offence which carries the risk of imprisonment for five years or more, and any attempt to commit such an offence, is now an arrestable offence. Powers of arrest under the Act are separately laid down according to whether an offence is about to be committed, or is in the course of being committed, or has been committed.

Offence about to be committed. A police officer, but not a private citizen, may arrest without warrant any person who is, or whom he, with reasonable cause, suspects to be, about to commit an arrestable offence.

Offence being committed. Any person may arrest without warrant anyone who is, or whom he, with reasonable cause, suspects to be, in the act of committing an arrestable offence.

Offence already committed. Where an arrestable offence has in fact been committed, any person may arrest without warrant anyone who is, or whom he, with reasonable cause, suspects to be guilty of the offence. In addition a police officer who, with reasonable cause, suspects that an arrestable offence has been committed may arrest without warrant anyone whom he, with reasonable cause, suspects to be guilty of the offence. The Act authorises reasonable force to be used and empowers a police officer (but not a private citizen) to enter and search any place where a person subject to arrest is suspected to be.

The Act of 1967 does not, of course, contain the whole law of arrest, or anything like it. That is not the way our law is organised. Numerous common law rules still apply, as laid down by the judges in various decisions. One important rule of this kind relates to the right of an arrested person to be told the ground on which he is arrested. Other rules state that where a private person carries out an arrest he must, as soon as he reasonably can, hand the wrongdoer over to a police officer. A common cause of private arrest is shoplifting, and it was established in a case concerning a shoplifter at John Lewis's Stores in Oxford Street that the store manager was not to be criticised because he held the shoplifter in custody for a while to consider the position before sending for the police. A police officer who arrests a person is entitled to do what is reasonable to investigate the matter and to see whether the suspicions which gave rise to the arrest are supported by the evidence. He can, for instance, take the person suspected back to his home to see whether any stolen property is there. If an alibi is offered, as that the suspect was at his place of work at the time in question, the police are entitled to take him there to check the alibi.

All that we have said about powers of arrest applies whether or not a warrant has been obtained from the magistrates. Indeed, the only real effect of a warrant is to protect the police officer effecting the arrest from an action for damages if the grounds for the arrest turn out to be mistaken. Most arrests have to be made quickly, without there being time to apply for a warrant. For the effective checking of crime, coupled with the safeguarding of the innocent, it is obviously desirable that the law regarding arrest without warrant should be clear and simple. The opposite is in fact the case.

Although we have attempted to summarise above the main rules governing arrest, it would be quite unsafe for anyone to rely on this summary. This is because there are in addition a large number of other powers of arrest, each having a slightly different effect, scattered throughout the Statute Book. J. D. Devlin listed 75 different statutory provisions conferring powers of arrest in his book *Police Procedure, Administration and Organisation* published in 1966. It cannot even be said that all these additional powers are related to special cases of narrow scope. One power, contained in an Act of 1851, gives a general power to arrest any person found committing an indictable offence by night. Most of these scattered powers are special, however, and a queer collection they make. A person who is cruel to an animal may be arrested under an Act of 1911, but if he chooses birds as his victims the power of arrest, expressed differently of course, is contained in an Act of 1954. An unlicensed pedlar is arrestable under the Pedlars' Act of 1871, but an unlicensed hawker falls to be dealt with under a different Act, of 1888. A female prostitute can be arrested for soliciting under the Street Offences Act, 1959; a male prostitute engaged in similar activities is arrestable under the Sexual Offences Act, 1956. The Acts just mentioned are part of the general law of the land, but the position is further complicated by the existence of many local Acts which only apply in limited areas. Some of these give very sweeping powers. Local Acts giving a general power to arrest a person found committing any offence whatever include the Salford Improvement Act, 1842, the Stockton-on-Tees Extension and Improvement Act, 1869, and the Birmingham Corporation (Consolidation) Act, 1883. Any reader who has cherished the faint hope that he might really get into his head the exact position concerning his rights and powers in relation to arrest will give up at this point. Unless, that is, he is prepared to confine his movements to areas where such local Acts have not been passed. Otherwise, on a simple journey from say London to Manchester his position will vary several times. Furthermore, the local Acts in question are virtually inaccessible, even to the ordinary lawyer. Most law libraries do not stock local Acts, and even if they did there is no published set of these which is up-to-date, comprehensive and fully indexed.

The complexity of the law of arrest does not stop here. Even a relatively simple provision may be expressed in terms of indictable offences only, and cannot be understood and applied without a knowledge of which offences are indictable and which are not. This is a complex study in itself. Until the Act of 1967 which abolished the distinction between felonies and misdemeanours the meaning of these terms might also have to be understood in order to apply arrest provisions. This was equally complicated. For this conundrum the Act substitutes another. It can only be applied by a person who knows which offences do, and which do not, carry five years' imprisonment. This is no less difficult to find out, and a list of the offences alters every year.

Another source of difficulty is the different wording of provisions having the same object. There are a number of enactments, dealing with such varying matters as protection of birds, dangerous drugs, elections and traffic offences, which confer powers of arrest intended to be limited to cases where the offender cannot be identified. The Acts in question are all of recent date, and yet there has been no consistency in the drafting of the provisions. One commentator, D. A. Thomas, remarks that 'it is difficult to see any logic or sound policy in these variations'. Equal difficulty arises in comprehending the policy of the Legislature in giving wider powers in cases which seem to be of lesser importance. For example, the power to arrest persons guilty of a highway obstruction is wider than the power to arrest those who commit indecent assaults on children.

It is obvious that these complexities and deficiencies of the law on the question of personal liberty are indefensible. They hamper the police in their work, and an officer faced with a critical situation is often compelled to act blindly in the hope that the law will support him. One detective inspector remarked that 'it is ludicrous to expect any police officer to carry in his head all his powers of arrest and the conditions appertaining to them. It is even more ludicrous to expect him to interpret them correctly when the courts themselves are at variance.' Professor P. J. Fitzgerald commented that it was intolerable that a handbook such as Devlin's *Police Charges* should have to use no less than seventeen different letters to symbolise the different powers of arrest applicable to the common offences. The position is no less serious for the private citizen. As D. A. Thomas remarked, he is seldom in a position to make even a tentative guess at his rights, either as a person threatened with arrest or as a private person attempting to effect the arrest of someone he sees committing an offence. Thomas goes on:

> The most reasonable and honest citizen, who would submit quietly to a lawful arrest (although innocent of the act for which he is being arrested), may become truculent and even violent when he believes he is being arrested unlawfully, and indeed the Law recognises his right to resist unlawful arrest by force.

At a time when the crime rate constantly increases, and citizens are officially encouraged to 'have a go' and join in the battle against the criminal, it is intolerable that the authorities responsible for the state of our statute law should allow these confusions and complexities to exist. We have been discussing arrest without warrant, but the law is hardly less complex in its application to the granting and effect of warrants of arrest. The need for reform is not so urgent here, however, as the issue of a warrant usually takes place in conditions allowing legal complexities to be investigated.

Apart from the defects of the law of arrest due to its complexity and inconsistency, the police themselves criticise it as inadequate. This particularly applies to relatively minor offences where the offender refuses to identify himself, and may go scot free if there is no power to arrest him. The Litter Act of 1958 made it a criminal offence to drop litter, but contained no enforcement powers. The result is that even where a person is seen by a policeman to throw litter in the street nothing can be done about it if he refuses to identify himself. The problems of the police where a suspect's identity is not known are illustrated by the 1966 case of *Rice* v.

Connolly. A police officer saw Rice behaving suspiciously in the early hours of the morning in an area where property had that night been broken into. Rice refused to answer any questions and would not agree to accompany the officer to someone who could identify him. He said, 'If you want me, you will have to arrest me'. The officer promptly complied with this suggestion, and charged Rice with obstructing him in the execution of his duty. It was later admitted by the police that Rice had no connection with the burglaries that night, and appeared to be an innocent person. In allowing Rice's appeal against conviction the Lord Chief Justice said:

> It seems to me quite clear that though every citizen has a moral duty, or if you like a social duty, to assist the police, there is no legal duty to that effect, and indeed the whole basis of the common law is the right of the individual to refuse to answer questions put to him by persons in authority, and to refuse to accompany those in authority to any particular place, short, of course, of arrest.

While no case has been made out for abrogating the principle of no self-incrimination, there does seem to be a justifiable case for requiring individuals to identify themselves when required by a police officer. Power to this effect has already been conferred in relation to identification of the driver of a motor vehicle, and it does not seem unreasonable to extend this generally. It perhaps should be further extended so that the police have adequate powers to check a proffered identification and to ensure that the person identified can be found if evidence incriminating him comes to light.

MISTAKEN IDENTITY

The most frequent cause of wrongful conviction is undoubtedly mistaken identity. Few people are observant enough to notice sufficient details about the appearance of a stranger to enable them to identify him later with certainty or give an accurate description of him. Especially is this so when the circumstances are unusual, as where the occasion for noticing a stranger is his commission of a criminal offence. A committee of inquiry into a famous case of mistaken identity, that of Adolf Beck, reported that evidence as to identity based on personal impressions was perhaps of all classes of evidence the least to be relied upon and, unless supported by other facts, an unsafe basis for the verdict of a jury. As Professor Glanville Williams has remarked in his book *The Proof of Guilt*, identification appears to be a matter on which personal pride has a strong effect. A witness often resents it when his ability to recognise someone is questioned. Once having made an identification he is reluctant to admit doubt.

The public mind is most exercised when there is a suspicion that a person has been executed for a crime he did not commit. Cases of this kind are few in British legal history, and in most of them innocence is merely a possibility and not a proved fact. One clear case was that of Jennings, who was executed at Hull in 1762 for theft following a mistake of identity. In modern times the execution of Hanratty for the A.6 murder caused considerable unease on grounds of identity. Celebrated cases where the victim was not executed, but was ultimately pardoned and compensated, include those of Adolf Beck, who was released after seven years' imprisonment, and Oscar Slater, who spent eighteen years in prison on a conviction for murder before it was officially admitted, after prolonged agitation, that his conviction was a mistake.

In our own day the case of P.C. Luckhurst led to improvements in the procedure for holding identity parades. Luckhurst was convicted of larceny of a bank wallet which had been found by a Colonel Manners in May 1966. He handed the wallet to one of two police officers who called at his house after he had reported the discovery. Some three months later it came to light that the wallet had not been handed in to the bank to which it belonged. Police inquiries followed and an identification parade was held at which Colonel Manners picked out P.C. Luckhurst as the man to whom he had handed the wallet. On Luckhurst's appeal, the Court of Criminal Appeal found that 'considerable improbabilities' arose over the case for the prosecution, but that equal if not greater improbabilities existed on the hypothesis that Luckhurst was innocent. The Home Office held an inquiry which brought to light procedural defects in the holding of identification parades. Criticism was aroused because the inquiry report was not published by the Home Office, and no action was taken to clear Luckhurst. In 1969, however, the Home Office published revised rules for the holding of identification parades. These emphasised that the object of the parade is to make sure that the ability of the witness to recognise the suspect is fairly and adequately tested. Witnesses must not be shown photographs of suspects if circumstances allow of a personal identification. If it is necessary to use photographs in order to get a description of a wanted man these should not be shown to all the witnesses, so that there remain some who, when the suspect has been apprehended, can be asked to pick him out at an identification parade without having seen his photograph beforehand. Where it is necessary to show a photograph of a suspect, it should be shown among other (unmarked) photographs having as close a resemblance to it as possible, and the witness should be left to make a selection without help and without opportunity of consulting other witnesses.

An identification parade is to be conducted by police officers having no connection with the investigation. Nothing must be done to draw attention to the suspect, who must be allowed to take up whichever position in the parade he chooses, and be placed in company with persons of similar appearance. Witnesses must not be allowed to communicate with each other. If a witness indicates someone but is unable to identify him positively, this must be recorded–as indeed must every other circumstance connected with the parade.

Despite all these precautions, identification remains a hazardous business. To a large extent this is inherent, and beyond the reach of procedural reforms.

COMPENSATING THE INNOCENT

There are other causes of possible miscarriage of justice apart from mistaken identity. A man may be wrongly convicted because of prejudice aroused through his bad character and previous convictions having been put in evidence, though this can usually only happen at the wish of the defence or through the accused having attacked the character of prosecution witnesses. Prejudice may also arise where several people, some of bad character, are involved in an incident and tried jointly. Perjured evidence is another possible cause of wrong conviction. Also, since the British system of criminal justice does not take the form of an inquisition into the truth but a contest between accuser and accused, the accused may go down unjustly if the case put forward on his behalf is inadequately prepared or mistakes are made in its presentation.

Since, therefore, there are possibilities, however remote, of mistaken conviction, it is important that a case should not be regarded by the authorities as closed once the trial and any appeal have been disposed of. Since the death penalty has been virtually abolished in Britain, the opportunity to remedy a miscarriage of justice remains after conviction. The police should therefore be encouraged to be alert for new evidence tending to show that a conviction is wrong. The Cross brothers owed their release to this sort of alertness by a police inspector. They had been convicted at Nottingham on the evidence of a woman who picked them out at separate identification parades as the men she had seen from an upper window attack and rob a chauffeur in a dimly-lit street. They vigorously protested their innocence at every opportunity but were convicted. After they had served eight months of their sentence a vigilant police inspector discovered that three other men later arrested for a similar crime were in possession of articles which the Cross brothers were supposed to have stolen. These men confessed to having committed the offence for which the Cross brothers had been convicted.

This case was cited by 'Justice' in a 1968 report urging more elaborate reviews of criminal convictions. This report urged that legal advice should be made available to prisoners in custody seeking to challenge the correctness of their conviction on the grounds of their innocence. The legal aid scheme should be extended to provide for this. Petitions from such prisoners should be taken more seriously by the Home Office, and only rejected if they are clearly without substance. In other cases an informal investigation should be carried out under the direction of a member of a panel of senior barristers and solicitors with experience of criminal cases. The services of independent persons able to conduct factual investigations should be made available for such inquiries. The resultant report should be available to the convict, and where it established the probability (even if not the certainty) of innocence a pardon should be granted. Where this type of inquiry did not resolve the matter a more formal hearing should take place before a commissioner of high authority with full power to examine witnesses and call for documents in the search for truth. The report also recommends fuller use by the Home Secretary of the power to refer cases after conviction to the Court of Appeal (Criminal Division) where points of legal difficulty are revealed.

What is to be done where a conviction is shown to be mistaken? Apart from the obvious justice of a free pardon and release from imprisonment, there is the question of compensation. The state has always been grudging in this matter. Adolph Beck, after seven years' wrongful imprisonment, was given a mere £5,000 as compensation. Oscar Slater was only given £6,000 after eighteen years' wrongful imprisonment. Ronald Avard, recently released from four years' detention in Rampton Mental Hospital with a Home Office apology after another case of mistaken identity came to light, was told that if he received compensation exceeding £1,650, he would cease altogether to receive the Social Security benefits paid since his release. Where society makes a mistake, however inadvertent, and inflicts this kind of unmerited punishment on one of its members it should, as a matter of law, make full restitution. The system of ex gratia payments should be replaced by a legal right to recover damages calculated on the basis of full restitution.

Hardship is not confined to the case where an innocent accused is convicted. Even if he succeeds in securing his acquittal he will often do so only at considerable expense and mental suffering. Here again, the state is extremely reluctant to provide compensation. It is true that many acquittals are obtained on technical rather than meritorious grounds; and there remains strong suspicion. Even where this is not so, however, an award of costs is unusual. When in 1969 Robert Winter, of the Tiger Club, was prosecuted for low flying and acquitted he was refused costs despite the plea that there was no evidence against him and it was obvious that the wrong man had been brought to court. The matter was subsequently raised in Parliament, but the Attorney-General saw no reason to intervene. In another case a youth charged with indecent assault was granted legal aid and assessed to a contribution of £55. The case against him collapsed and he was acquitted, but he was still ordered to pay his contribution. The position is difficult to rectify without introducing the possibility of a verdict of innocent, as opposed to a finding of not guilty. Here again the accusatorial system of British justice impedes a fair solution. Perhaps all that can be done is to encourage the court to be more generous in its awards of costs to persons acquitted of crime, and to give them as a matter of course when complete innocence is established.

TAILPIECE: BINDING OVER

The British pride themselves on living under the rule of law. Dicey, the great constitutional lawyer, expressed this in the form 'no man is punishable or can be lawfully made to suffer in body or goods except for a distinct breach of law established in the ordinary legal manner before the ordinary courts of the land'. It is possible, however, for a person who has committed no offence to suffer in body or goods where magistrates invoke the power to bind over conferred by an Act of Edward III. This enables a single justice to order a person against whom no criminal charges have been preferred to enter into recognisances and find sureties to keep the peace; and if he refuses, to send him to prison for up to six months. The National Council for Civil Liberties called in 1969 for the repeal of this ancient power. Although upheld by some as a piece of preventive justice, and undoubtedly having its uses, the Act does not fit into present day concepts of the treatment of the individual. Binding over may not be a punishment but it undoubtedly carries a stigma, as shown by the fact that applicants for posts in Government service are sometimes asked to state whether they have ever been bound over. The Home Office were therefore wise in responding promptly to the request by the National Council for Civil Liberties and ordering an inquiry to determine whether the power to bind over need be retained.

10

Inquiries, Tribunals and Ombudsmen

In previous chapters we have been concerned with the effect on the individual of ordinary legal rules and procedures. We turn now to another topic–administrative law. The impact of this is if anything more widespread. In fact we are each of us much more likely to be affected by administrative actions and decisions than to be the subject of ordinary legal process. These still involve tangling with the law, since administrative powers are conferred and regulated by statute, but it is a different kind of law. It is mainly operated by civil servants and uses machinery fully developed only very recently. We look now at that part of this machinery which aims to ensure that administrative decisions are fair to the citizen and properly within the powers conferred by Parliament.

PUBLIC INQUIRIES

Good administration depends on adequate knowledge as a basis for decisions. Avoidance of public dissatisfaction depends on giving objectors a chance to let off steam, and showing that all relevant views on a proposed course of action have been taken into account. It is for these reasons that public inquiries are held, and they have become a common feature of post-war life in Britain. They are particularly used to enable views to be aired on land proposals: compulsory acquisition, development schemes, and other projects relating to the use of land.

The usual sort of public inquiry is conducted in the area where the matter arises by a civil servant, called an inspector, from the Government department concerned. The holding of the inquiry will have been advertised in local newspapers, and interested parties and organisations will have been notified well in advance. Objectors and others wishing to put forward views may appear in person or by lawyers. Evidence may be given and witnesses cross-examined as in court. The inspector makes a written report to his Ministry recording the evidence, his findings of fact and his recommendations. The report is considered within the Ministry by a civil servant of appropriate seniority and a decision given on it. Only matters of the highest importance come before the Minister personally.

Recent improvements in procedure now require such reports to be published, or at least made available to interested parties. On issues of law the Minister is required to give a reasoned decision, which the courts may review. In certain cases the holding of an inquiry is compulsory, but more usually it is held at the discretion of the Minister. Failure to order an inquiry sometimes gives rise to criticism, as do other aspects of the inquiry procedure. Where permission is refused by a local planning authority on an application to develop land an appeal lies to the Minister. The number of planning applications is not far short of half a million a year, and appeals are brought in about fifteen thousand of these cases. The backlog of such appeals varies, but delays may be as much as nine months or a year. Occasionally complaints arise because new evidence has been considered by the Minister after the closing of the inquiry. This happened in the Packington Estate affair in 1967, when a contest arose as to whether an area in Islington should be redeveloped or should be renovated. Against the advice of his inspector the Minister decided in favour of renovation. Undeterred, the would-be developers (who were the local council) applied again for planning permission and this was granted without an opportunity for objection being given those who had appeared at the inquiry on the previous application.

A similar case giving rise to widespread dissatisfaction was the Stansted Airport inquiry. The procedure adopted by the Government in relation to the proposed development of Stansted as the third London Airport was the subject of many complaints. Objections to the original proposals were the subject of a public local inquiry in 1965/66. The Inspector urged that a review of the whole matter should be undertaken by a committee equally interested in traffic in the air, traffic on the ground, regional planning and national planning, and that the review should cover military as well as civil aviation. This recommendation was not made known to the objectors, and was only published at the time the Government announced its decision to give permission for development of Stansted Airport. Public concern increased when a few months later the Government proposed a realignment of the runways in a way which meant that a different set of local residents would be differently affected, some more seriously than before, and some for the first time. The Government proposed to make this change without holding a further inquiry. Prompted by the large volume of complaints, the Council on Tribunals made a special report stating that, as a matter of justice, all whose lives and property would be seriously affected by the change should be given the opportunity of a fair hearing of their objections at another public inquiry. Subsequently the proposals for Stansted were dropped, and the whole question of the siting of London's third airport thrown open for fresh consideration.

The Council on Tribunals was set up in 1958 on the recommendation of the Franks Committee. Its function as a watchdog over inquiries was at first limited to those which were held compulsorily, but this limitation was removed in 1966. The Council has worked well, but some critics feel its powers should be further strengthened. It is argued that it should be able to bite as well as bark; that is have power to take positive action against abuses. It seems doubtful whether this is necessary; the instances of abuse are rare, and no case has arisen where criticism by the Council has failed to effect the necessary improvement in administrative procedures.

As its name indicates, the Council is mostly concerned with the supervision of administrative tribunals. These differ from inquiries in a number of ways. Both are fact-finding bodies, but the inquiry forms part of a larger procedure whereas the tribunal carries out a complete operation. Having found the facts it decides the case by applying legal rules. The decision is the tribunal's own, and the Minister is not responsible. The issue before an inquiry will ultimately be decided by the Minister (or officials acting for him), and the purpose of the inquiry is to ensure that the decision is taken on full information. While inquiries are part of the machinery of administration, tribunals, it has been held, should properly be regarded as machinery provided by Parliament for adjudication.

THE GROWTH OF ADMINISTRATIVE TRIBUNALS

When the Council on Tribunals got to work in 1959, it found that it had assumed jurisdiction over about two thousand tribunals exercising thirty-five different functions and hearing well over 100,000 cases a year, most of them involving disputes between a private individual and a Government department. The main area of jurisdiction is the welfare of the individual: his health, his employment, his income and his home. The key to the growth of tribunals undoubtedly lies in the concept of the Welfare State as developed since the last war. Professor H. W. R. Wade has called them a by-product of an age of intensive government:

> Less and less are people left to rely on personal transactions enforced by the law courts. More and more are they made subject to regulatory schemes–national insurance, the health service, state education, agricultural control, rent control and many other such things are administered under elaborate Acts of Parliament. Here is a new source of social friction, for there are bound to be many disputes.

When the state provides a variety of benefits for its citizens it clearly has to devise machinery for determining whether a claimant is entitled to participate, and if so to what extent. This job could have been left to the ordinary courts, and it is interesting to see why this was not done. In a nutshell, the post-war administrative schemes depended for their successful working on an adjudication procedure which was quick, cheap, informal and flexible; and had due regard to social factors. The courts could not offer these qualities. Nor did the administrators who had to work the schemes feel that lawyers, with their conservative outlook, had the initiative to supply them. As Lord Evershed, himself a distinguished lawyer, put it, a reason for the growth of tribunals was 'undoubtedly an impatience with the expense, the delays and the formalities of the ordinary courts. In other words, the mistrust of the law was in large measure a mistrust of legal procedure.' Not only, therefore, was adjudication under novel measures such as the National Health Service Act entrusted to tribunals, but the courts were deprived of jurisdiction they had previously enjoyed–for example in workmen's compensation cases. As Professor Harry Street put it: 'If the average claim to benefit is less than £10, we do not want a judge on a pensionable salary of £8,500 a year with all the trappings . . . of special judges' lodgings, private butler, police escort, ushers, and marshal, to decide the claim. Nor do we want years to elapse between the making of the claim and the arrival of a final decision.'

Adjudication is often needed on matters requiring technical knowledge, and tribunals can be staffed by specialists. Barristers have always resisted the appointment of anyone not of their number as a judge, and even expert assessors are frowned upon. Lawyers selected as judicial material usually come from upper middle class backgrounds, and are felt by many social reformers to lack concern for the problems of the poor and ignorant. Lawyers are often excluded from any participation in tribunal proceedings–even as advocates. The effectiveness of tribunals stems largely from speedy and informal procedure, which cannot survive the arts of advocacy and cross-examination. The Council on Tribunals has found that tribunals do all they can to ensure that parties do not suffer through having to appear in person rather than with legal representation. 'We have also formed the impression from our visits to tribunals that Chairmen, while recognising the importance of representation in appropriate cases, are against anything that might complicate the existing arrangements. . . .'

The lack of representation before tribunals explains why it has not been thought necessary to provide legal aid. Parties need help most often where the complications of land law are involved, and there has been much pressure for some form of legal aid before the Lands Tribunal. The Council feel, however, that there is a greater need for some form of assistance by surveyors. The professional societies recently launched a pilot Surveyors' Aid Scheme under which surveyors give their services on terms similar to those governing legal aid to tenants and landlords concerned in appeals to rent assessment committees. The pilot scheme operates only in the London area, but may well develop into something of a social importance comparable to legal aid. Certainly there is no reason why the legal profession should be alone in offering this kind of assistance on terms by no means beneficial to itself.

CONTROLLING THE TRIBUNALS

In the early days of administrative tribunals their procedure often bore no resemblance to that regarded as essential by a court of law for the protection of the parties. In one case, where a Board of Trade tribunal dealt with a disciplinary charge against a patent agent, the court before whom its decisions were ultimately brought remarked that the tribunal was composed of individuals who did not need to possess any judicial or other appropriate qualifications. It conducted its investigations in private; it had no power to compel the attendance of witnesses or the production of documents; it could not administer an oath, and had no rules of procedure; it communicated no findings or decision to the parties; it made a report to the Board which was conclusive as to the facts, but of which no copy was furnished to accuser or accused; and there was no appeal. Lord Justice Farwell had once stated that he could not trust the whole Bench of Bishops to do justice under such conditions. The judge trying the case commented:

> With a respect for the episcopate as profound as that of the Lord Justice, I entirely adopt his language. I share to the full his distrust of justice, administered by a tribunal sitting in private unassisted and untrammelled by the salutory rules regulating procedure and the admission of evidence obtaining in these courts, uncontrolled by the invigorating and corrective criticism provoked and stimulated by publicity, and finally wrapping up its findings in a secret communication to the Department which appointed it.

It took many years for views like this to take effect. Growing distrust of the rough-and-ready procedure of administrative tribunals led to the appointment in 1955 of the Franks Committee, which reported that tribunals should show the three basic characteristics of openness, fairness and impartiality. Provided this were done there would be no need to yield to the pressure to transfer the jurisdiction of tribunals to the ordinary courts. Indeed the committee found positive advantages in not doing this, for if a large number of disputes dealt with by tribunals were handed over to the courts there would have to be a considerable increase in the number of judges and this would lead to a lowering in the standards of the administration of justice. The committee concluded that the system of administrative tribunals 'has positively contributed to the preservation of our ordinary judicial system'.

The Council on Tribunals, set up as a result of the Franks Committee, is required to keep under review the constitution and working of tribunals and to report on them annually to Parliament. When it receives a complaint about the procedure of a tribunal it investigates the complaint and if necessary makes representations to the governmental body concerned. As we have seen, it has no compulsory powers, but any criticism it makes is attended to immediately. When the Council condemned the practice of rent tribunals deciding cases without inspecting the interior of the premises the practice was immediately changed. When a ratepayer who had appealed to a local valuation court against his rate assessment complained that the valuation officer was chatting to members of the court before the hearing whereas the ratepayer had to stay outside in the waiting-room, the department concerned undertook to see that this kind of apparent unfairness was not repeated.

There is in theory a system of judicial control over the actions of tribunals. Certainly if they infringe the statutory rules governing the tribunal in question, the courts can intervene on the application of an aggrieved party. There are two problems in the way of this being an effective remedy. One is that the Act setting up a tribunal usually makes it difficult, and occasionally impossible, for the court to take action. Appeals, where they exist, are normally restricted to questions of law, whereas grievances often arise on questions of fact. The other difficulty is that the legal procedure for review is encrusted with antiquated technicalities. As the Law Commission have recently remarked, the procedural complexities which face the litigant who seeks an order of certiorari, prohibition or mandamus have long been the subject of criticism. Not only has the law been by-passed by the growth of tribunals; it has failed to keep up to date its machinery for controlling them.

THE OMBUDSMAN (PARLIAMENTARY COMMISSIONER)

When the terms of reference of the Franks Committee were announced, Professor J. A. Griffith lamented that the enquiry had been directed exactly in the wrong direction. The existing procedures for inquiries and tribunals were already predominantly open, fair and impartial. There was, he thought, a much greater need for inquiry into what went on inside Government departments. Into these 'closed, dark and windowless procedures' the Franks Committee was not asked to let air and light. A Report by 'Justice' in 1961 called for this omission to be rectified by the appointment of an ombudsman authorised to investigate complaints of maladministration. This suggestion was adopted a few years later.

The office of ombudsman was first created in Sweden, where it was set up as long ago as 1809. The need existed there because under the Swedish system civil servants are not, as in Britain, subject to the control of Ministers. The ombudsman supervises the activities of officials, and has power to prosecute those who act illegally or in neglect of their duties. This system did not provide any control over decisions taken by officials without maladministration. This was rectified by the setting up in 1909 of a General Tribunal. Other countries to appoint an ombudsman are Denmark (in 1955) and New Zealand (in 1962). The advice of the New Zealand ombudsman, Sir Guy Powles, was sought when Britain decided to follow suit.

The British ombudsman, established in 1967, was given the title Parliamentary Commissioner. The Government did not, however, follow the 'Justice' recommendation and also set up a General Tribunal on the lines of the Swedish body. The Commissioner is a servant of the House of Commons, which has set up a permanent select committee to supervise his activities. Naturally enough, the Commissioner began cautiously and operated at first on a fairly narrow front. Encouraged by the select committee, however, he broadened the scope of his work and his powers as currently applied offer very great help to the citizen who is the victim of official ineptitude or unfairness. The following rules show the powers and limitations of the Commissioner, and are worth bearing in mind by anyone who wishes to have a grievance investigated:

1. A case can only be referred to the Commissioner by a Member of Parliament. All this means is that instead of writing to the Commissioner direct a complainant should write to his own Member of Parliament asking for the matter to be referred to the Commissioner.

2. The Commissioner can only deal with complaints of maladministration by Government departments. This means that he cannot deal with a complaint against a local authority, the police, a nationalised industry, or a hospital.

3. Normally a complaint cannot be entertained unless it is made to a Member of Parliament within twelve months of the date on which the complainant first had notice of the matter complained of. The Commissioner has a discretion to waive this time limit if there are special circumstances.

4. The Commissioner cannot investigate a grievance if there is a right of appeal to a court or tribunal.

5. The Commissioner cannot investigate complaints by civil servants themselves relating to their appointments or other relationships with their employer.

6. A complaint cannot be entertained against the operation of an Act of Parliament where no administrative discretion is involved.

7. The Commissioner will not entertain a complaint unless it is made by the aggrieved person himself, that is, the person against whom the official action in question was taken. It is therefore not enough that the grievance is felt by a person as an ordinary citizen or taxpayer. So where a complainant had helped an alien and his family to get permission to enter Britain but subsequently found the alien to be of bad character, the Commissioner could not

entertain his complaint when the Home Office, disregarding his representation, allowed the alien to remain in the country.

The Parliamentary Commissioner receives about 2,000 complaints every year. The majority of these are rejected as being beyond his jurisdiction or not made through Members of Parliament. In 1968 the number of cases for which a complete investigation was carried out was only 374. The Ministry about whom most complaints were received was the Department of Health and Social Security, which had more than double that of any other department. Next came the Ministry of Housing and Local Government and the Inland Revenue. The reports of the Commissioner show the very high standard of administration in the British Civil Service. Cases of serious maladministration are very rare indeed; instances of *deliberate* unfairness are practically unheard of. The cases illustrated in the report give a fascinating picture of the working of our Civil Service and the variety of ways in which administrative action impinges on the citizens. It is not possible to give here more than a small selection of these.

We have discussed in Chapter 3 the need of the citizen for advice about the laws that beset him and have argued that in matters within the province of a Government department it is the responsibility of the Department to ensure that people are aware of their rights and liabilities. Many cases brought to the Parliamentary Commissioner concern this aspect. The law relating to retirement pensions is complex, for example, and many people are unsure of their rights. Nevertheless the law says that no pension is payable unless claimed. Notwithstanding this it is quite rightly the practice of the Department of Health and Social Security to remind people, shortly before they reach normal retirement age, to make a claim for their pension. They do not send reminders in all cases, however, and sometimes a reminder fails to reach the person concerned, or is overlooked by him. The resultant financial loss is in law the pensioner's own fault, and the Commissioner is helpless. Post war credits give rise to similar problems. One complainant alleged that the Inland Revenue had refused to allow interest on post war credits of her late husband who had died in 1949. The

Revenue had advised her, as was then correct, that she would not be entitled to payment of the credits for many years. They did not notify her when the law was changed in 1959, entitling her to immediate payment. Nor would they allow her any interest for the period during which the credits were retained after they could have been paid. The Commissioner rejected the claim of maladministration on grounds which are of general interest:

> My investigation shows that the Inland Revenue receive a large number of enquiries about post war credits, and other aspects of tax law, and their practice is to answer on the basis of the current law. They have represented to me that it is impossible for them to accept responsibility for reviewing their files after every change in the law, to see if their past replies require correction. It must be recognised that there are severe practical limitations to what can be done, and, provided adequate publicity is given to changes which may affect taxpayers' interests, I do not think that I can contest the view of the Inland Revenue that it would not be reasonable, even if it were administratively feasible, for the Department to take the initiative in informing individuals that information given at some earlier date was no longer correct.

Another advice case concerned a fireman injured in the course of his duties. A medical board made a final assessment of disablement benefits to be paid until a date in 1958, by which time it was expected he would make a full recovery. He did not do so and in 1960 asked at the Ministry whether he was entitled to any further benefit. He was told that as the medical board's assessment had been final, there was no question of further compensation. This was wrong, since the medical board could have been asked to reopen the case. After inquiries by the Commissioner they agreed to do this, and the matter was put right. Sometimes wrong advice leads to a payment of *ex gratia* compensation. This happened when a Customs and Excise Office delayed answering a firm's query as to whether they could get a refund of duty on oil they were supplying at a duty-free price to a customer entitled by law to receive fuel oil free of duty. It was ultimately held that a refund was not payable, and the firm suffered considerable loss. The department offered an *ex gratia* payment of some £440, which was about one-third of the loss. The company complained that this was insufficient, but this was rejected by the Commissioner on the ground that the firm itself was mainly at fault since it took the business risk of carrying on with the contract while having strong reason to think it would do so at a loss. The Customs Officer concerned had not encouraged it to take this risk, and the department were if anything being generous in the compensation offered. Compensation of this kind is not usually offered by a Government department: in this case it arose because duty had been paid which if the parties had gone about the matter the right way would not in law have been payable.

Complaints are frequently made about planning decisions. Usually these are beyond the powers of the Commissioner, since the responsibility for day to day administration of planning control is laid by statute on the local planning authorities whose actions are outside his jurisdiction. The Ministry do possess reserve powers, and complaints can be made to the Commissioner where they decline to exercise them. It is Ministry policy to use their power to intervene only where the issue is one of more than local importance or raises a fundamental planning principle. The Commissioner has accepted the soundness of this policy, and treats complaints accordingly. Where, however, the development in question is carried out by a Government department the Commissioner can intervene. One complaint concerned a proposal by the Ministry of Technology to convert a private house in a residential area into a hostel for 23 young apprentices. The Commissioner rejected the complaint, partly on the ground that 'a former resident had kept monkeys, both in the house and in the garden'! Quietness and privacy are regarded as important by most people, and one man went so far as to complain to the Commissioner that private personal information about him had been improperly used by a driving examiner in failing him for the tenth time. The complainant was much older than he looked, being in fact in his middle sixties. Age is not required to be declared when applying for a driving test, and the complainant suspected that knowledge of his age had reached the examiner by unofficial means and had influenced his decision. The Commissioner found this was not so.

Our other examples of decisions by the Parliamentary Commissioner relate to matters even more keenly felt–freedom of action and personal liberty. The hobby of collecting coins seems harmless enough, but in one case before the Commissioner a numismatist complained that his hobby was being impeded by the refusal of the Bank of England to allow him to acquire post-1837 gold sovereigns. This was done under legislation designed to stop hoarding and speculation in gold coins. Although authorised collectors are exempted, the question whether an applicant is an authorised collector is judged by criteria which, because of the risk of abuse, are not published. The complainant alleged that the rejection of his application was an infringement of personal liberty, but since the restriction was in accordance with legislation approved by Parliament the Commissioner felt unable to intervene. Another case concerning freedom of action arose when an Englishman living in Wales complained about compulsory Welsh lessons for his children. The subject was mainly within the powers of the local authority, and there was little the Commissioner could do. The matter had been brought to the Ministry, who had limited power to intervene, but there was no maladministration in their decision not to do so. The parent invoked a provision in the Education Act of 1944 instructing the Minister to have regard to the principle that so far as possible pupils are to be educated in accordance with the wishes of their parents. The Commissioner found that due weight had been given to this.

Finally we look at two cases involving personal liberty. In the first, a prisoner complained that, despite a confession by his ex-wife that she was responsible for the frauds for which he was convicted, the Home Office refused either to investigate the matter or to allow him to start legal proceedings against her. The first part of the complaint was outside the Commissioner's jurisdiction, and the Commissioner found no maladministration in the refusal to allow the prisoner to start proceedings. The policy of the Home Office is not to allow prisoners to attempt to bring a private prosecution against witnesses at their trial or other persons connected with the case. It was not for the Commissioner to question this policy. It is perhaps open to question, but this would have to be done by ordinary political action in Parliament or elsewhere. In the other case a Magistrates' Court, on the application of the Inland Revenue, had granted a warrant for the committal of the complainant to prison, suspended for one month, for the non-payment of income tax. In fact, errors had been made by the Inland Revenue and there was no tax liability. They apologised to the complainant, reimbursed her expenses, and took steps to ensure that effect was never given to the committal order. The complainant wanted the committal order quashed, but Counsel advised that there was no way of doing this. It might, however, be possible to get leave to appeal out of time, and the Inland Revenue offered to meet the costs. The Commissioner found that the combination of errors which gave rise to the case, and for which the Inland Revenue accepted the full blame, were due to human failures and not to any basic weakness in procedures. While the complainant had a grievance, the Inland Revenue had done everything in their power to remedy it.

These cases, which are a typical selection, show that the dark corners of administration referred to by Professor Griffith contained nothing very sinister after all. Within the field allotted to him, the Parliamentary Commissioner performs a useful and effective role. The obvious question is whether this field should be widened. The Government have accepted in principle that an ombudsman system should be by law established for investigating complaints of maladministration by local government. This announcement, made in 1969, received a mixed reception. What, it was asked, are elected councillors for, if not to investigate grievances? Is there really any need to set up a new state organisation to probe the activities of local councils and their officials? There seems little evidence of widespread dissatisfaction with the quality of local government administration, given the financial limitations within which it must operate. The need is for less, rather than more, bureaucratic organisation. If evidence of abuses cannot be produced it is pointless to create elaborate machinery for their removal.

CAN LAW STAGE A COME-BACK?

As we have seen, administrative tribunals have grown up because legal process was felt to be inadequate to serve administrative ends. On top of this, the supervision of administrative tribunals, and indeed the administrative processes of central government generally, have been entrusted not to legal process but to bodies working in the same way as the administrators themselves. This victory of administration over law has been consolidated by the obvious success of the methods used. They are effective, and they are fair. What more can anybody want?

The only thing wrong with this state of affairs is that the rule of law, upon which British liberties are supposed to depend, has gone out of the window. The rule of law requires people to be given definite rights which the court will enforce. The convenience of administration is better served by conferring discretion upon officials, and avoiding legal process. On the one hand people know their rights, and can enforce them in open court; on the other, much depends on quiet conversations behind closed doors. The one process is lengthy and expensive, the other is quick and efficient. Under present-day conditions in Britain both are equally fair, but can this kind of administrative system ensure that fairness continues–or is it basically unsound?

Lawyers have for some time been uneasy about the decline of legal principles. In a paper issued in 1969 the Law Commission uttered a clarion call to lawyers to regroup and re-equip their forces. The Parliamentary Commissioner, they said, is a supplement to, rather than a substitute for, a comprehensive and coherent system of administrative law. '. . . the institution of that important office in no way diminishes the need for a review of the legal redress available in respect of administrative actions.' There is need, in the opinion of the Law Commission, for a single form of legal procedure for reviewing acts and omissions of the administration. Special legal remedies may need to be created where the individual is opposed to a Government department. It may be necessary to recognise in the fields of contract and tort that the Government as a party is different from a private party and, as in a number of other countries, provide special rules of public law accordingly. Judges sitting for this purpose may need to be specially trained in techniques of administration. The Law Commission therefore calls for an inquiry into administrative law by a Royal Commission, or body of similar status.

The Parliamentary Commissioner, in his report for 1968, records the case of a complainant who was dissatisfied by the decision of the Minister on his appeal against an enforcement notice. The Commissioner rejected the complaint because there was a right to challenge the Minister's decision in the High Court on a point of law. The complainant had not exercised this right, no doubt because the trouble and expense involved were too much for him to contemplate. He would have been much better off if the right had not existed, since then the Commissioner would have investigated the case, and if the grievance was justified action would have been taken to remedy it. This example shows what those who seek to revive the rule of law in the administrative field are up against. Even if they succeed they are likely to find that most people will prefer to have their grievances investigated by a person who, like the Parliamentary Commissioner, can act informally, can inspect Ministry files without restriction, and can pursue his enquiries by letter, telephone and personal call with speed and effectiveness. While standards of public life are what they are today in this country such methods are likely to prove the most acceptable. At all events, if a system of administrative law is introduced it should not interfere with the citizen's right to elect, if he wishes, to have his grievance against central Government investigated by the method now open to him.

11

Priorities for Reform

In the previous chapters we have looked briefly at some of the points at which law and the citizen make contact, and at reforms recently made or currently proposed. The treatment could not be exhaustive in a book of this size, and no attempt has been made to deal with reforms which are in the pipeline–for example the overhaul of the system of circuits and assize courts which is being considered by a Royal Commission under Lord Beeching. We have concentrated on the individual, with sympathy for his problems in struggling to keep within the law and avoid its harsher consequences. The reader is not likely to have found the result of the examination entirely reassuring.

In the course of a brief survey we have glimpsed some important principles that need to be safeguarded. There can be little doubt that the most important of these is the independence of the legal profession itself. Without this the citizen cannot be assured of impartial advice in time of trouble. It is not too much to say that the preservation of this independence, from which stems the independence of the courts themselves, is the only sure protection against state tyranny. The danger of undermining legal independence is real and immediate. It is all the more potent because it comes mostly from within. Independence is threatened not by would-be tyrants seeking to abolish an obstacle in their path to autocratic rule, but by a small number of reforming lawyers. These are genuinely concerned at the plight of poor people who lack ready recourse to legal advice. The intentions of these reformers are undoubtedly good, but as a great Viceroy of India once said, in assessing the consequences of a proposed course of action there can be no allowance for good intentions.

There are many other important principles which in these days are at risk. The rule of law itself is threatened by the growth of administrative tribunals and procedures which often bypass the courts. Beguiled by the speed and simplicity of administrative procedures for redress of grievances, society may overlook the risk involved in setting aside safeguards that only courts of law can provide. Nevertheless much needs to be done before judicial control can resume its rightful place.

This brings us to another great question. How can court procedure be simplified so as to give a really effective reduction in the time and cost of litigation? Can the oral procedures of our courts survive? Should entirely new devices, such as a speedy trial on written material only, be introduced? It seems that only by such means can a serious blot on our system of procedural law be removed. This is the injustice caused when the individual has to forgo his rightful claim because the consequences of pursuing it are too daunting to contemplate.

In the field of criminal law we have seen other great questions emerge. Are our reformers right to abolish the concept of guilt for children and adolescents? When shall we see remedied the iniquity of a law of arrest so complicated and confused that neither the police nor anyone else can hope to grasp it? Should we permit abrogation of the rule that no man is obliged to incriminate himself, and compel our citizens to answer police questioning?

Underlying questions concern the whole future of law as we know it. Law tends to be a black and white concept. Either a right exists or does not. A man is guilty of crime or he goes scot-free. Social development may come to regard these concepts as too crude a means of regulating a community. Social relationships may be seen more and more as indeterminate, the subject for discretionary action rather than predetermined rights and duties. Protection is being given more and more through the principle of social security and less by reliance on private rights of action. This applies particularly in the field of protection against loss due to personal injury or ill health. Some reformers even advocate that we should abolish altogether the law of tort so far as it relates to personal injuries and switch to a state insurance system. In New

Zealand changes of this kind have already been proposed by a Royal Commission.

Lawyers may be left high and dry as society seeks different ways of securing the benefits that legal rules and legal process should provide. More and more areas may be withdrawn from legal purview, as we have seen happening with the treatment of young offenders and with the adoption of the maxim 'Don't litigate–insure'. Those with power effectively to decide these matters (mainly Civil Service administrators) are likely more and more to push the boundaries of administration into legal territory. So long as legal process remains subject to the grave deficiencies we have discussed the citizen will not protest at the enlargement of administrative boundaries; on the contrary he will demonstrate his support for simpler procedures and choose arbitration instead of litigation whenever he can. Perhaps this is the way we are destined to go, and perhaps society will not in the long run suffer. The risk is there, however, and it is for lawyers to ensure that it is not embarked on willy-nilly through avoidable failures to reform legal process.

A lot of reform is undoubtedly going on. Much thought is devoted to the subject–both by official agencies such as the Law Commission and by unofficial bodies like 'Justice'. Few reforms are really comprehensive, however, and there is little sign of thorough planning. Many ramshackle parts of our legal system are allowed to creak along without serious attention. When a body like the Payne Committee produces a thoroughgoing and comprehensive reform of a particularly bad area we are pleased, but find the operation unusual. Our reformers seem to lack a sense of priorities, and to be too much concerned with 'lawyers' law'. Anomalies in substantive rules that have irritated lawyers for years may be swept away with advantage. But it would perhaps be better to devote our scarce resources in money and manpower to a truly radical overhaul of procedure, and the framework of law. There is undoubtedly much more wrong with the procedure than with the substance of our law. The biggest scandal of all is the state in which the laws themselves are presented to those who have to use them.

No official inquiry has ever been made into the waste of time and money arising from the fact that law is not processed so as to be easily consulted and understood. Computers and other scientific aids are waiting to be used. The first priority of all is a thoroughgoing official examination into the whole system of statute law–its preparation, enactment, publication, amendment and use. The tidying up of statute law must no longer be hamstrung by lack of Parliamentary time. Parliament must, to safeguard the rule of law itself, facilitate the consolidation and updating of statute law by authorising joint committees of both Houses of Parliament to decide by a simple procedure whether proposed minor changes are acceptable. If changes pass the committee, they should not have to run the gauntlet of all other stages in Parliament. This reform, coupled with an energetic programme of recruitment and training of draftsmen, could clear the way for production of the first properly organised Statute Book this country has ever had.

Finally, our lawmakers might ponder the wise words of Lord Darling: 'Men would be great criminals did they need as many laws as they make.' We should be able to look forward to a time when at least our basic laws are regarded as settled, so that the citizen has a chance to study and learn them. In the relatively tranquil state of society in Britain the pursuit of legal reform should not need to be a permanent activity. It will, however, on any view, be a necessary activity for a considerable time to come.

APPENDIX 1

Advisory Services

There follows a list of sources of advice to the public. The first mentioned are Citizens' Advice Bureaux and Members of Parliament, and then the list gives a few examples of institutions which fall under a number of different categories. Wherever possible the addresses and telephone numbers are provided, together with a brief description of the nature of the advice, and who may benefit from it.

CITIZENS' ADVICE BUREAUX

Address and telephone no.–local.

General advice: will usually put persons in touch with lawyer. Bureaux are organised on a local, self-governing basis or run by Councils of Social Service and other voluntary organisations on behalf of the supervising body, the National Council of Social Service.

MEMBERS OF PARLIAMENT

Local address and telephone number, and
House of Commons
Westminster
London S.W.1. Tel: 01-930 6240

GOVERNMENT BODIES

(Advice available to all–quality of advice differs widely between Departments and offices.)

Agriculture, Fisheries and Food (Ministry of)
Local address and telephone number, and
Whitehall Place
London S.W.1 Tel.: 01-839 7711

Board of Trade
Local address and telephone number, and
1 Victoria Street
London S.W.1 Tel.: 01-222 7877

Charity Commission
14 Ryder Street (St. James's)
London S.W.1 Tel.: 01-930 7621
Advice to charity trustees on matters affecting charities.

College of Arms
Queen Victoria Street
London E.C.4 Tel.: 01-248 2762
Advice on the law relating to heraldry, arms, etc.

APPENDIX I

Customs and Excise Department
Local address and telephone number, and
King's Beam House
Mark Lane
London E.C.3 Tel.: 01-626 1515

Defence (Ministry of): Army Legal Services Department
Lansdowne House
Berkeley Square
London W.1 Tel.: 01-499 8040
For members of the services abroad, unable to deal satisfactorily with cases at home.

Employment and Productivity (Department of)
Local address and telephone number, and
8 St. James's Square
London S.W.1 Tel.: 01-930 6200

General Register Office
Somerset House,
Strand
London W.C.2 Tel.: 01-836 2407
and
Fermanagh House
Ormeau Avenue
Belfast Tel.: Belfast 27311
Advice on registration, e.g. births, deaths, marriages, special procedures, etc.

Health and Social Security, Department of
Local address and telephone number, and
10 John Adam Street
London W.C.2 Tel.: 01-930 9066

Home Office
Local address and telephone number, and
Whitehall
London S.W.1 Tel.: 01-930 8100

Inland Revenue
Local address and telephone number, and
Somerset House
Strand
London W.C.2 Tel.: 01-836 2407

Nationalised Industries' Consumers Councils
e.g. Electricity Consultative Council, Transport Users Consultative Committee – local addresses and telephone numbers: also Telephone Users' Association, 35 Connaught Square, London W.2 Tel.: 01-262 5988.

Patent Office, and Industrial Property and Copyright Department
25 Southampton Buildings
London W.C.2   Tel.: 01-405 8721
Advice on patent law, copyrights, etc.

Post Offices
Local address and telephone number. Advice on matters within the sphere of the Minister of Posts and Telecommunications.

Probate Registry
Local address and telephone number, and
Somerset House
Strand
London W.C.2   Tel.: 01-405 7641
Advice on wills and estates: procedures, etc.

Public Trustee Office
24 Kingsway
London W.C.2   Tel.: 01-405 4300
Advice relating to estates for which the Public Trustee is responsible.

Registrar General's Office
New Register House
Edinburgh   Tel.: 031-556 3952
Advice on registration, e.g. births, deaths, marriages, special procedures, etc.

Royal Air Force Legal Services
Turnstile House
High Holborn
London W.C.1   Tel.: 01-405 6977
For members of the service abroad, unable to deal satisfactorily with cases at home.

Scottish Office (and its administrative departments)
Dover House
Whitehall
London S.W.1   Tel.: 01-930 6151
and
St. Andrew's House
Edinburgh 1   Tel.: 031-928 8501
(and local offices in Scotland)

Treasury, Solicitor's Department
3 Central Buildings
Matthew Parker Street
London S.W.1   Tel.: 01-930 1124

Welsh Office
47 Parliament Street
London S.W.1   Tel.: 01-930 3151

APPENDIX I

Local Government Departments

The following departments of local authorities offer advisory services from their local offices:

Children's Departments. Should be able to help regarding legal enquiries about children.

Health Departments. Personnel should be acquainted with the law in their particular fields.

Housing Departments. Should be able to help with legal enquiries in their sphere.

Police Forces (and individuals thereof). Policemen are often highly knowledgeable in particular branches of the law.

Probation and After-Care Services. Probation officers knowledgeable and helpful with some experience of dealing with marital problems.

Town Clerks' Departments. In large authorities may house a legal department as such. Usually the starting point for general enquiries.

Welfare Departments. Personnel should be acquainted with the law in their own particular fields.

Motorists' Associations

Automobile Association
Fanum House
Leicester Square
London W.C.2   Tel.: 01-930 1200
Advice for members only, of a limited nature.

Royal Automobile Club
89 Pall Mall
London S.W.1   Tel.: 01-930 2345
Advice for members only, of a limited nature.

Newspapers' and Magazines' Advice Bureaux

Fenton Bresler
c/o *She* Magazine
Chestergate House
Vauxhall Bridge Road
London S.W.1   Tel.: 01-834 2331
Advice free to all readers.

The John Hilton Bureau
News of the World
30 Bouverie Street
London E.C.4   Tel.: 01-353 3030
Advice free to all readers.

The John Noble Reader's Service
Sunday Mirror
33 Holborn
London E.C.1 Tel.: 01-353 0246
Advice free to all readers.

The Reader's Advice Service
The People
96/98 Long Acre
London W.C.2 Tel.: 01-836 1200
Advice free to all readers.

PROFESSIONAL AND TRADE ASSOCIATIONS

Examples of the many which provide advice to their members are:

Association of British Chambers of Commerce
68 Queen Street
London E.C.4 Tel.: 01-248 7211

British Dental Association
63 Wimpole Street
London W.1 Tel.: 01-935 0785

British Medical Association
B.M.A. House
Tavistock Square
London W.C.1 Tel.: 01-387 5601

County Landowners' Association
7 Swallow Street
London W.1 Tel.: 01-734 2712

General Nursing Council
23 Portland Place
London W.1 Tel.: 01-580 3898

National Chamber of Trade
3 Hyde Park Place
London W.2 Tel.: 01-262 3061

National Farmers' Union
Agriculture House
Knightsbridge
London S.W.1 Tel.: 01-325 5077

Royal Institute of British Architects
66 Portland Place
London W.1 Tel.: 01-580 5533

Royal Institute of Chartered Surveyors
12 Great George Street
London S.W.1 Tel.: 01-930 5322

APPENDIX I

Social Welfare Organisations

Abortion Law Reform Association
19 Kenneth Court
173 Kennington Road
London S.E.11 Tel.: 01-735 7166
Advice on abortion law and procedure.

Agnostics Adoption Society
69 Chaucer Road
London S.E.24 Tel.: 01-274 2407
Advice on adoption law (non-sectarian).
(There are a number of other adoption societies, and some are of a sectarian nature.)

Albany Trust
32 Shaftesbury Avenue
London W.1 Tel.: 01-734 5588
Pressure group 'to promote psychological health': legal advice given.

The British Legion
49 Pall Mall
London S.W.1 Tel.: 01-930 8131
For members and certain others (ex gratia).

Catholic Marriage Advisory Council
Clitherow House
15 Landsdowne Road
London W.11 Tel.: 01-727 0141
Advice on marital problems, basically but not exclusively, Roman Catholic.

Family Service Units
Local address and telephone number. These units will give advice about domestic problems.

Family Welfare Association
Denison House
296 Vauxhall Bridge Road
London S.W.1 Tel.: 01-834 7334
London based, and the principal association of its kind: many others similar in other regions.

Marriage Guidance Councils
Local address and telephone number, and
58 Queen Anne Street
London W.1 Tel.: 01-935 2838
Advice available to all on marital problems.

National Council for Civil Liberties
4 Camden High Street
London N.W.1 Tel.: 01-387 2544
May advise in cases relevant to its interests, e.g. cases before the Mental Health Review Tribunal.

National Council for the Single Woman and her Dependants
166 Victoria Street
London S.W.1 Tel.: 01-828 5511
Advice for single women with elderly persons to look after.

National Council for the Unmarried Mother and her Child
255 Kentish Town Road
London N.W.5 Tel.: 01-485 8383
Advice for the single mother.

The Patients' Association
335 Gray's Inn Road
London W.C.1 Tel.: 01-837 7241
Advice of medico-legal nature regarding, for example, legal rights arising from maltreatment.

Soldiers', Sailors' and Airmen's Families Association
27 Queen Anne's Gate
London S.W.1 Tel.: 01-839 4131
Advice of limited nature for servicemen and ex-servicemen and their families.

Trade Unions

Generally speaking, unions will provide legal advice to members only in respect of matters arising in connection with their employment, and not, for example, regarding domestic family problems. Examples of unions which provide advice are:

National Union of Mineworkers
222 Euston Road
London N.W.1 Tel.: 01-387 7631

National Union of Seamen
Maritime House
Old Town
London S.W.4 Tel.: 01-622 5581

National Union of Teachers
Hamilton House
Mabledon Place
London W.C.1 Tel.: 01-387 9191

Voluntary Legal Advice Centres

There are several free legal advice centres; addresses may be obtained from local authorities, Citizens' Advice Bureaux, etc.; those in London include:

APPENDIX I

Cambridge House Legal and Family Advice Centre
137 Camberwell Road
London S.E.5 Tel.: 01-703 3051

Islington Legal Advice Centre
Unity Church Hall
Upper Street
London N.1

The Mary Ward Centre Legal Advice Department
9 Tavistock Place
London W.C.1 Tel.: 01-387 8271

Release
52 Pricedale Road
London W.11 Tel.: 01-229 7753
Advice of general nature catering for all age-groups, but largely oriented towards the problems of the young.

Toynbee Hall Legal Advice Centre
28 Commercial Street
London E.1 Tel.: 01-247 4172

University House Legal Advice Centre
Victoria Park Square
Bethnal Green
London E.2 Tel.: 01-980 4204

OTHER MISCELLANEOUS BODIES

Other bodies exist which may be able to advise specific categories of persons or in relation to particular kinds of problems. These include:

Clerks to the Justices and Court Offices
Advice on procedures, etc.

Criminal Injuries Compensation Board
19 Woburn Place
London W.C.1 Tel.: 01-837 0479
For victims of criminal assaults in the line of public duty.

Education, The Advisory Centre for
57 Russell Street
Cambridge Tel.: 0223-51456
Advice on matters of education.

Law Society's Legal Aid Office
Advise locally in operation of state schemes.

Legal Departments and Personnel Officers in Commerce and Industry

Motor Insurers' Bureau
Aldermary House
Queen Street
London E.C.4 Tel.: 01-248 4477
For victims of road accidents in financially adverse circumstances.

The Poor Prisoners' Defence Fund (The National Association for the Care and Resettlement of Offenders)
125 Kennington Park Road
London S.E.11 Tel.: 01-735 1151
For persons charged with a crime where, e.g., other aid is not available. Advice on procedures, etc.

Race Relations Board
St. Stephen's House
Victoria Embankment
London S.W.1 Tel.: 01-930 6322
For victims of racial discrimination.

Rent Officers (local)

FURTHER REFERENCE

Further reference should also be made to Appendix II of the author's book *Professional Ethics*. This describes the services which may be obtained by the public from practitioners in the consultant professions. Such practitioners are often highly knowledgeable about the law relating to their own particular fields.

APPENDIX II

Select Bibliography

1. BOOKS

Abel-Smith, B. and Stevens, R., *Lawyers and the Courts*, Heinemann, 1967.

Bennion, F. A. R., *Professional Ethics: the consultant professions and their code*, Charles Knight, 1969.

Derriman, J., *Pageantry of the Law*, Eyre and Spottiswoode, 1955.

Devlin, J. D., *Police Procedure, Administration and Organisation*, Butterworth, 1966.

Devlin, Lord, *Trial by Jury*, Stevens, 1966.

Driedger, E., *The Composition of Legislation*, the Queen's Printer, Ottawa, 1957.

Jackson, R. M., *The Machinery of Justice in England*, C.U.P., 1967.

Megarry, R. E., *Lawyer and Litigant in England*, Stevens, 1962.

——, *Miscellany-at-Law*, Stevens, 1958.

Street, H., *Freedom, the Individual and the Law*, 2nd ed., Penguin, 1967.

——, *Justice in the Welfare State*, Stevens, 1968.

Walker, N., *Crime and Punishment in Britain*, Edinburgh Univ. Press, 1965.

Williams, G., *The Proof of Guilt*, 3rd ed., Stevens, 1963.

Zander, M., *Lawyers and the Public Interest*, Weidenfeld & Nicolson, 1968.

2. OFFICIAL REPORTS

1949. *Report of the Committee on Depositions*, Cmd. 7639.
Report of the Committee on County Court Procedure (Austin Jones Report), Cmd. 7668.

1949 and 1953. *Reports of the Committee on Supreme Court Practice and Procedure* (Evershed Report), Cmd. 7764 and 8878.

1957 *Report of the Committee on Tribunals and Inquiries* (Franks Report), Cmnd. 218.

1962 *Report of the Committee on Consumer Problems* (Molony Report), Cmnd. 1781.

1965. *Report of the Departmental Committee on Jury Service* (Morris Report), Cmnd. 2627.

1966. *Report of the Departmental Committee on Legal Aid in Criminal Proceedings* (Widgery Report), Cmnd. 2934.

1967. *Seventeenth Report of the Law Society on Legal Aid and Advice*, 1966-7.
Annual Report of the Council on Tribunals.

1967 and 1968. *Annual Reports of the Parliamentary Commissioner for Administration.*

1968. *Report of the Committee on Personal Injuries Litigation* (Winn Report).
Third Annual Report of the Law Commission.
Report of the National Board for Prices and Incomes on Remuneration of Solicitors, Cmnd. 3529.
Children in Trouble, Home Office, Cmnd. 3601.
Report of the Committee on Local Authority and Allied Personal Social Services (Seebohm Report), Cmnd. 3703.

1969. *Report of the Committee on the Enforcement of Judgment Debts* (Payne Report), Cmnd. 3909.
Administrative Law, Law Commission, Cmnd. 4059.
Identification Parades, Home Office.

3. PAMPHLETS AND ARTICLES

1966. 'The Anti-Social Child in Care', *Annual Review of the Residential Child Care Association.*
'Police Powers', by D. A. Thomas, *Criminal Law Review*, December.
Some Suggestions on the Form and Publication of Statute Law, by F. A. R. Bennion (unpublished).

1968. 'Codification of the Law of Contract', by A. L. Diamond, *Modern Law Review*, July.
Home Office Reviews of Criminal Convictions, 'Justice'.
Justice for All, The Society of Labour Lawyers, Fabian Society.
The Parliamentary Threat to Freedom, by P. De La Cour.
Rough Justice, by a Committee of Conservative Lawyers, Conservative Political Centre.
Searching Law by Computer, by J. F. Horty.

1969. *Civil Appeals–Proposals for a Suitors' Fund*, 'Justice'.

Index

INDEX